SELF-DEFENSE

Steps to Success

Joan M. Nelson, MA
Director, Movement Arts, Inc.
Lansing, Michigan

Leisure Press
Champaign, Illinois

Library of Congress Cataloging-in-Publication Data

Nelson, Joan M., 1949-
    Self-defense : steps to success / Joan M. Nelson.
        p.   cm. -- (Steps to success activity series)
    Includes bibliographical references (p.).
    ISBN 0-88011-430-4
    1. Self-defense. I. Title. II. Series.
    GV1111.N46   1991
    613.6'6--dc20   90-25460
                                                                CIP

ISBN: 0-88011-430-4

Acquisitions Editor: Brian Holding
Developmental Editor: Judy Patterson Wright, PhD
Assistant Editors: Kari Nelson, Dawn Levy, and Julia Anderson
Copyeditor: Sam Cogdell
Proofreader: Dianna Matlosz
Production Director: Ernie Noa
Typesetters: Brad Colson and Kathy Boudreau-Fuoss
Text Design: Keith Blomberg
Text Layout: Tara Welsch
Cover Design: Jack Davis
Cover Photo: Wilmer Zehr
Interior Art: Tim Offenstein, Gretchen Walters
Printer: United Graphics

Instructional Designer for the Steps to Success Activity Series: Joan N. Vickers, EdD, University of Calgary, Calgary, Alberta, Canada.

Leisure Press books are available at special discounts for bulk purchase for sales promotions, premiums, fund-raising, or educational use. Special editions or book excerpts can also be created to specification. For details, contact the Special Sales Manager at Leisure Press.

Printed in the United States of America

10 9 8 7 6 5 4 3 2

Leisure Press
A Division of Human Kinetics Publishers, Inc.
Box 5076, Champaign, IL 61825-5076
1-800-747-4457

Canada Office:
Human Kinetics Publishers, Inc.
P.O. Box 2503, Windsor, ON N8Y 4S2
1-800-465-7301 (in Canada only)

Europe Office:
Human Kinetics Publishers (Europe) Ltd.
P.O. Box IW14
Leeds, LS16 6TR
England
0532-781708

Contents

The Steps to Success Activity Series is a breakthrough in skill instruction through the development of complete learning progressions—the *steps to success*. These *steps* help students quickly perform basic skills successfully and prepare them to acquire advanced skills readily. At each step, students are encouraged to learn at their own pace and to integrate their new skills into the total action of the activity, which motivates them to achieve.

The unique features of the Steps to Success Activity Series are the result of comprehensive development—through analyzing existing activity books, incorporating the latest research from the sport sciences and consulting with students, instructors, teacher educators, and administrators. This groundwork pointed up the need for three different types of books—for participants, instructors, and teacher educators—which we have created and together comprise the Steps to Success Activity Series.

The *participant book* for each activity is a self-paced, step-by-step guide; learners can use it as a primary resource for a beginning activity class or as a self-instructional guide. The unique features of each *step* in the participant book include

- sequential illustrations that clearly show proper technique for all basic skills,
- helpful suggestions for detecting and correcting errors,
- excellent drill progressions with accompanying *Success Goals* for measuring performance, and
- a complete checklist for each basic skill for a trained observer to rate the learner's technique.

A comprehensive *instructor guide* accompanies the participant's book for each activity, emphasizing how to individualize instruction. Each *step* of the instructor's guide promotes successful teaching and learning with

- teaching cues (*Keys to Success*) that emphasize fluidity, rhythm, and wholeness,

- criterion-referenced rating charts for evaluating a participant's initial skill level,
- suggestions for observing and correcting typical errors,
- tips for group management and safety,
- ideas for adapting every drill to increase or decrease the difficulty level,
- quantitative evaluations for all drills (*Success Goals*), and
- a complete test bank of written questions.

The series textbook, *Instructional Design for Teaching Physical Activities*, explains the *steps to success* model, which is the basis for the Steps to Success Activity Series. Teacher educators can use this text in their professional preparation classes to help future teachers and coaches learn how to design effective physical activity programs in school, recreation, or community teaching and coaching settings.

After identifying the need for participant, instructor, and teacher educator texts, we refined the *steps to success* instructional design model and developed prototypes for the participant and the instructor books. Once these prototypes were fine-tuned, we carefully selected authors for the activities who were not only thoroughly familiar with their sports but also had years of experience in teaching them. Each author had to be known as a gifted instructor who understands the teaching of sport so thoroughly that he or she could readily apply the *steps to success* model.

Next, all of the participant and instructor manuscripts were carefully developed to meet the guidelines of the *steps to success* model. Then our production team, along with outstanding artists, created a highly visual, user-friendly series of books.

The result: The Steps to Success Activity Series is the premier sports instructional series available today. The participant books are the best available for helping you to become a master player, the instructor guides will help you to become a master teacher, and the teacher educator's text prepares you to design your own programs.

This series would not have been possible without the contributions of the following:

- Dr. Joan Vickers, instructional design expert,
- Dr. Rainer Martens, Publisher,
- the staff of Human Kinetics Publishers, and

- the *many* students, teachers, coaches, consultants, teacher educators, specialists, and administrators who shared their ideas—and dreams.

Judy Patterson Wright
Series Editor

This book provides an integrative approach to dealing with physical aggression and verbal threat. The unique progression of skills is intended to help you develop greater awareness and vigilance, hone observational and judgment skills, learn communication techniques to defuse potentially volatile situations, and acquire competency in physical self-defense tactics for use when preventive measures fail.

This particular progression of skills, referred to as the *Continuum of Response*, reflects my belief that prevention and postponement of physical aggression are critical self-defense skills. Hence, the first 3 steps focus on strategies and skills to be implemented before the onset of physical aggression, that is, *before* you are grabbed, shoved, punched, or hit.

Another concept integrated into this book and related to the notion of doing everything possible to postpone or prevent aggression is the *ethic of least harm*. This is the principle, written into law, that requires that we use *only* that amount of force that is reasonable and necessary to protect ourselves and others. The initial defensive maneuvers in this book are designed to neutralize the attack (not the attacker) when physical defense is deemed necessary. And counterattacks (offensive techniques) should be used only when purely defensive techniques are no longer sufficient to maintain your safety.

Another unique aspect of this book is the emphasis on training mind and emotions as well as the body. A recurring theme is the development of "recall under stress," that capacity for clear and strategic thinking in responding to the emergency of assault. Within each step, progressively more challenging and realistic drills help you to increase your ability to maintain presence of mind, to make accurate observations, to determine possible options and risks, and to select effective and appropriate choices for defense. The final chapter, entitled "Recall Under Stress," stretches even further your ability to remain focused while resisting the panic and confusion that frequently characterize assaultive situations.

This book is written for beginning level students in self-defense. For this reason, it is heavily weighted toward prevention and defense against unarmed attacks. Special assaultive situations, such as dealing with multiple attackers or armed attackers, will not be covered.

However, the section "Epilogue: The Next Step" provides suggestions for selecting a martial art style and school for those who want to go beyond this introductory training in self-defense. Basic self-defense courses, such as the one offered here, bear the same relationship to martial arts study as first aid training does to the field of medicine. For more intensive and extensive training, commitment to long-term study of a martial art is usually necessary.

For those less interested in ongoing training, but concerned about some of the issues raised in this book, the epilogue also offers encouragement and suggestions for joining national or local community groups working in a variety of ways to reduce violent victimization.

I would like to acknowledge a number of people who have directly and indirectly contributed to this book. First I would like to thank Dr. Nancy Van Noord, Dr. Jayne Schuiteman, and Saundra Dunn for reading portions of the manuscript and giving me thoughtful and valuable advice.

The portion of the book on Confrontation/Assertiveness builds on the pioneering work of Sunny Graff and the Columbus, Ohio–based Women Against Rape (1983). Other portions reflect the insights and ideas of many other members of the National Women's Martial Arts Federation, especially the innovative and excellent work of Jaye Spiro of Detroit, Michigan (1988).

Thank you, Eileen Roraback, for your generous assistance with the portion of this book dealing with sexual assault, and Kris Metheny and Mark Nelson for your patience "under the lights" during our long photography sessions.

I owe a great debt to my parents, Otis and

the late Eva Nelson, who encouraged me to develop the skills I would need to live my life as I chose.

And finally, thank you to Deb Wieber, Ginny Hambric, and Fred Warren for your perspicacity, your vision, and your boundless encouragement in this and every other Movement Arts venture.

Joan M. Nelson

The Steps to Success Staircase

Get ready to climb a staircase—one that will lead you to greater knowledge and skill in maintaining personal safety. You cannot leap to the top; you get there by climbing one step at a time.

Each of the 14 steps you take is an easy transition from the one before. The first three steps will introduce you to the three A's of Personal Safety—Awareness, Assessment, and Action—and to strategies aimed at *preventing* physical aggression.

As you progress through these critical steps, you'll become more aware of the dynamics of assault and become familiar with typical characteristics of assailants and victims of various forms of aggression. You'll learn how to evaluate a potentially dangerous situation or person quickly and accurately, and then you'll learn verbal and psychological skills for preventing potential assaultive situations from escalating to the point of physical violence.

In Steps 4 through 13 you'll learn techniques for defending yourself when all efforts at prevention fail. The first half of these introduce you to solid fundamental skills, such as evasions, blocks, and counterattacks. Further on, you will have the opportunity to apply these basic skills as you learn effective responses to a number of common unarmed attacks.

A final step, entitled "Recall Under Stress," takes you even further in developing a capacity for clear and stategic thinking in dealing with the emergency of assault. Here a series of drills helps you develop the ability to maintain sufficient presence of mind to assess a rapidly changing situation, determine options and risks, and select and implement appropriate defenses.

To prepare yourself to begin this climb, read the sections on "Self-Defense Today" and "Preparing Your Body for Success" very carefully. Then follow this sequence each step of the way:

1. Read the explanations of what is covered in the Step, why it's important, and how to execute or perform its main focus, which may be a basic skill, concept, tactic, preventive strategy, or combination of these.

2. Follow the numbered illustrations showing exactly how to position your body to execute each basic skill successfully. There are three general parts to each skill: preparation (the starting position for each defense), execution (performing the skill that is the focus of the step), and follow-up (retreating from danger or continuing one's defense).

3. Look over the common errors that may occur and the recommendations of how to correct them.

4. Read the directions and the Success Goal for each drill. Practice accordingly and record your score. Compare your score with the Success Goal for the drill. You should meet the Success Goal for each drill before moving on to practice the next one because the drills are arranged in an easy-to-difficult progression. The drill sequence also enables you to test your mastery of basic technique in increasingly realistic practice situations. In this way, you can measure your performance quantitatively against the Success Goal while you increase confidence in your ability to execute these skills under stressful and often confusing circumstances.

5. When you've met all the Success Goals for a particular step, you're ready for a qualified observer—such as your teacher, coach, or trained partner—to evaluate your skills. This is a qualitative, or subjective, evaluation of your ability to execute each strategy or technique presented.

6. Repeat these procedures for each of the 14 Steps to Success. Then rate yourself according to the directions in the "Rating Your Total Progress" section.

7. Read the "Epilogue" section and determine your *next step*.

As you practice the skills presented throughout this book, remember that the study of self-defense is serious but not necessarily grim or somber. Let yourself have fun and enjoy this confidence-building journey of self-discovery and empowerment!

Key*

Ⓐ = attacker

Ⓓ = defender

⟶ = direction of attacker's movement

- - - ➤ = direction of defender's movement

Note: Because only a small number of the violent crimes committed are reported to authorities, it is impossible to determine precisely the proportions by sex and race of those involved. The "attackers" (A) and "defenders" (D) featured in the illustrations reflect a composite of current government statistics and independent research on perpetrators and victims of violent crime.

Self-Defense Today

Self-defense training has changed considerably over the years. Once the nearly exclusive concern of law enforcement and military personnel and students of martial arts, this training has become much more popular with the general public concerned about the rising incidence of crimes of violence.

TRAINING INNOVATIONS

Consequently, the nature of the training has changed as well. Although it once consisted almost entirely of learning physical techniques drawn from various martial disciplines, today's self-defense training is often much more integrative—combining observational, judgment, communication, and physical self-defense into one comprehensive program.

Ideally, self-defense training today involves

- deepening your understanding about the nature and prevalence of violent behaviors,
- learning how to assess risk and vulnerability rapidly and realistically in different circumstances,
- examining your behaviors and habits to determine how they impact your "victim potential,"
- developing more verbal and nonverbal skills for de-escalating a potentially explosive situation, and finally
- learning to respond with appropriate physical tactics, but only after you've learned all you can about prevention and avoidance.

It has been said about self-defense training that fully half of what we learn is preventive, and we practice it in hopes of never having to use the other half.

Self-defense training today can challenge us emotionally and transform us by revealing our emotional responses to threat and aggression. In the process of learning these skills, you may find yourself bumping up against fear and sometimes anger, or perhaps discovering an unexpected capacity for determined and spirited resistance to victimization. Learning these skills can be tremendously empowering —contradicting, as it does, messages of victimization and powerlessness that may be a part of your experience.

Today's self-defense is often specialized in order to meet the needs of particular groups or populations. For instance, unique self-defense programs focusing on the particular concerns, strengths, and vulnerabilities of women and children are now offered in most major cities. This has come about as a result of the efforts of many in the women's movement to increase awareness of sexual assault, spouse battering, and child sexual abuse over the last two decades.

Comprehensive self-defense programs have also been developed for professionals whose jobs bring them into contact with potentially explosive individuals, among them mental health professionals, hospital emergency room staff, social workers, and parole agents. These programs invariably take into account the unique job circumstances, relationships with clients, and safety concerns of human service workers.

Classes have been developed by and for people with disabilities. These training programs capitalize on the strengths while compensating for possible limitations of people in wheelchairs (see Figure 1), or those with hearing or visual impairments.

Avoidance and prevention of assault are a major concern for all of these groups. Skills and behaviors designed to postpone physical aggression are emphasized. Physical techniques, while an essential part of the training, are seen as a backup and used when all efforts at preventing physical aggression fail.

CONTINUUM OF RESPONSE

This philosophy of pushing back the moment when you're forced to resolve a situation with physical aggression is reflected in the Continuum of Response shown in Figure 2. Notice that the Continuum moves from *Awareness*

Figure 1. This drawing shows Ron Scanlon, master and eighth degree black belt in kung fu san soo and self-defense coordinator, Casa Colina Community Wheelchair Sports Program, in action. Based on a photo by Teresa Whitehead, courtesy of Casa Colina Centers for Rehabilitation.

and *Assessment* to *Action*. These three A's of Self-Defense represent major decision levels in maintaining personal safety.

Awareness refers to your knowledge about just what it is that you're learning to defend yourself against. It is the sum total of information you have accumulated about the nature, circumstances, stages, and psychodynamics of various forms of interpersonal aggression and threat. The more knowledgeable you are about these things, the greater the likelihood of your *avoiding* nasty situations entirely.

Assessment refers to the process of quickly and accurately evaluating a specific situation in which you feel at risk. In contrast to Awareness, which refers to general background knowledge and experience, Assessment is immediate, rapid, and situation-specific. The more skillful you are in reading dangerous situations and people, the more likely you are to extricate yourself before violence occurs.

Action results from the interplay of Awareness and Assessment and is based on an understanding of strategies for defense and their potential outcomes. You'll notice that under "Action" on the Continuum, three of the four strategies presented in this book involve actions taken *before* the onset of physical aggression—before you are grabbed, shoved, or punched. These three strategies, as well as information about Awareness and Assessment, will be covered in Steps 1 through 3. *Self-Defense*, the fourth and final point on our Continuum of Response, refers to strategies and tactics used in response to actual physical attack. These tactics will be the focus of Steps 4 through 14.

Continuum of Response

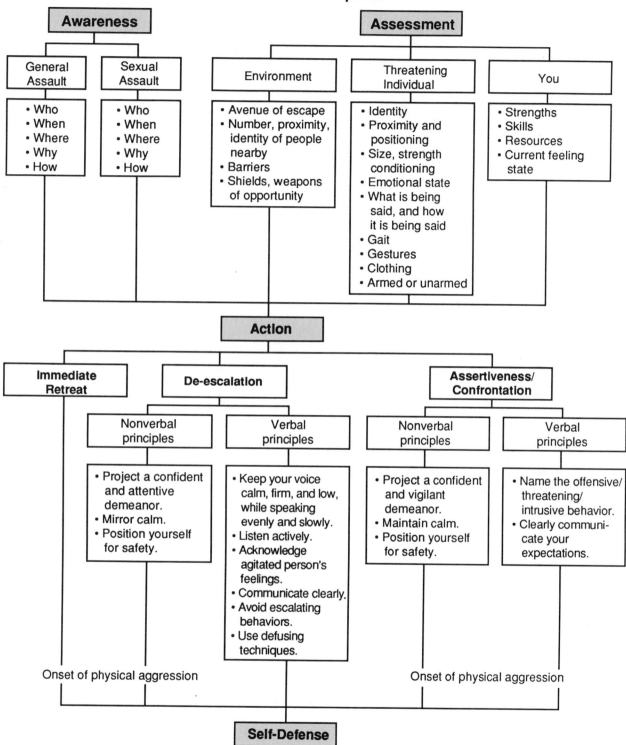

Figure 2. Continuum of response.

Preparing Your Body for Success

Warm-ups and cool-downs are needed in self-defense, as in most physical activities and sports. Emphasis in our warm-up is on first increasing heart rate for a few moments in preparation for the flexibility and strength exercises that follow. The cool-down consists of simply repeating the flexibility exercises done in the warm-up.

You'll be doing a series of stretches and strength-building exercises that focus initially on the large, central muscles of the trunk, and then move to smaller, peripheral muscles. When doing any of these exercises, pay attention to sensations arising in the muscles involved. For instance, focus on relaxing around the sensation of stretch. Allow the stretch to take place, let go into it. This enables you to let go of tension and resistance, increase range of motion, and center yourself.

Be as mindful of sensation during strength-building. Be aware of especially weak or strong areas. Learn to distinguish between muscle fatigue and muscle pain. Stop, of course, when you feel the latter.

Correct breathing during stretching and strength-building is an important part of each exercise. Exhale as you move into each stretch, and then hold for a count of 10. Take care not to bounce during a stretch. Instead keep still when you reach full extension. For the strength-building exercises, exhale on effort and avoid any jerky or sudden movements.

WHY ARE PROPER WARM-UPS AND COOL-DOWNS IMPORTANT?

Proper warm-ups prepare the body for the powerful trunk rotations and ballistic movement frequently employed in self-defense. Flexibility allows you to move through the wide range of motion that is characteristic of many self-defense techniques, and strength-building allows you to do so quickly and powerfully. Not surprisingly, adequate warm-ups significantly reduce the likelihood of injury during practice.

Stretch cool-downs reduce postpractice muscle soreness, and leave your body (and mind) in a more relaxed state.

The long-term effect of regular stretching and strength-building exercises is to improve your general state of health and well-being. This, of course, will affect your ability to muster the physical and the emotional resources that you need to defend yourself in the event that you are ever attacked.

HOW TO WARM-UP AND THEN COOL-DOWN

Our warm-up can be divided into three phases (see Figure 3). The first phase consists of approximately 3 minutes of mild aerobic activity to increase circulation and raise the temperature of your blood and muscles. The second phase focuses on flexibility and consists of a series of stretches. The third phase consists of a sequence of strength-building exercises.

The cool-down simply involves repeating the second phase, the flexibility segment, at the close of your workout.

Figure 3 Keys to Success: Warm-Up and Cool-Down

Phase 1: Preliminary Phase

1. Increase circulation
2. Increase temperature of blood and muscles

Phase 2: Flexibility Exercises

Work from large to small and from central to peripheral muscle groups

1. Trunk/Back
2. Shoulders
3. Legs
4. Neck

Phase 3: Strength-Building Exercises

Work from large to small and from central to peripheral muscle groups

1. Trunk/Abdomen
2. Legs
3. Shoulders/Arms/Hands

Phase 4: Cool-Down
Repeat Phase 2.

EXERCISES TO PREPARE YOUR BODY FOR SUCCESS

Begin each workout session with all three phases. Do 3 minutes of mild aerobic exercise, followed by the stretch sequence and then the strength-building sequence. Close your workout with the cool-down stretches that make up Phase 2.

Phase 1: Preliminary Phase

To prepare your body for stretching and strength-building, do 3 minutes of one of the following mild aerobic exercises:

1. Jogging in place
2. Jumping jacks (moderately paced)
3. Brisk walking

Phase 2: Flexibility Exercises

Take 8 to 10 minutes to work through the following 7 stretches. Remember to do them slowly and carefully. Keep in mind that stretching is not a matter of teeth-gritting effort. Rather, it involves letting go . . . of effort, tension, and resistance.

Trunk/Back

1. Trunk Rotations
   Stand with your legs slightly more than shoulder-width apart, and begin slowly to rotate around a vertical axis. Arms should be bent at right angles and held away from the body at shoulder height. After 15 seconds of continuous rotation from side to side let your arms straighten and swing freely in the direction of the rotation. Allow your head to turn easily

from side to side as you swing your arms. Continue rotations for about 30 seconds more with arms swinging freely.

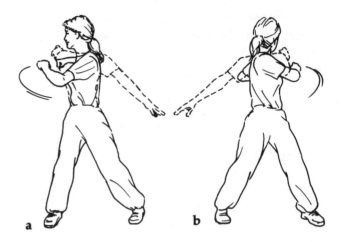

a   b

2. Side Stretches
   Stand erect with feet slightly more than shoulder-width apart. Reach straight up with your right arm, leaving your left arm dangling at your side. Reach as far upward as you can, while exhaling. Keep breathing as you hold your maximum stretch for a count of 10. Slowly release, and repeat on the other side.

3. Six-Count Body Curl
   Inhale deeply as you extend both arms straight overhead. Keep your gaze focused on your hands and let your extended arms drift slowly downward until you're bending forward at the waist. Bend only as far as flexibility *comfortably* permits, and make sure your knees are slightly bent at all times. To ensure that you're exhaling while bending, count out loud to six.

   Hold this position for a few seconds, then slowly roll back up, vertebra by vertebra. As you rise back up, inhale deeply and draw your hands along a plane in front of and close to your body. Finish by standing erect with arms once again extended overhead. Repeat stretch once more.

Shoulders

4. Arm Circles
   Slowly move your extended arms in large circles, 10 times forward and then 10 times in a backward direction. You're

a

b

c

d

a

b

actually circling your shoulder joint, reaching as far as possible to achieve as wide a range of motion as shoulder flexibility permits. Synchronize movement with breathing so that you're inhaling while lifting your arms and exhaling as you lower them.

5. Arm Sweeps
   Standing erect with feet slightly more than shoulder-width apart, sweep your extended arms along a horizontal plane at shoulder height. Move both arms simultaneously toward, then away from the body's centerline. Synchronize movements with your breathing so that you're inhaling as you move your arms laterally and exhaling as you move them across the front of your body.

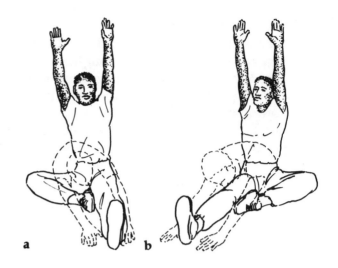

Legs

6. Hamstring Stretch
   Assume a modified hurdler's stretch, with one leg extended in front of you and the other bent so that your heel tucks into your groin. Take a deep breath as you reach straight overhead with both arms. Then as you exhale, slowly reach out and over your extended leg in the direction of your toes. Go as far as flexibility comfortably permits, hold for a few seconds, and then slowly release. Repeat once more on the same side, and then repeat the exercise on the other side.

Neck

7. Five-Direction Neck Stretch
   In a seated position with your back erect, allow your chin to drop slowly forward toward your chest. Hold for 1 second and then return your head to its vertical axis. Then let your head fall gently to the side, imagining that you're trying to touch your shoulder with your ear, hold it there, and then return your head to a vertical axis. Let your head drop to the opposite shoulder, hold for a few sec-

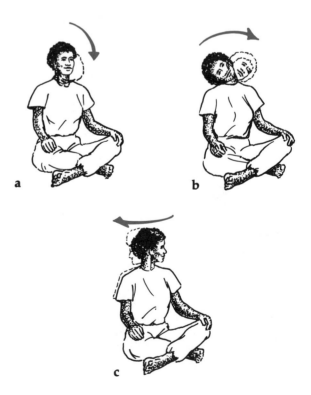

onds, and then return. Finally, rotate your head as if looking over your shoulder at something behind you. Be sure to maintain a vertical axis, leading with your chin and not your crown. Do this in each direction, taking care to hold for only a couple of seconds before returning your head to the neutral starting position. As you stretch your neck in each of the five directions, be sure to exhale. Inhale as you return to the neutral position, that is, to a vertical axis. Also, keep your trunk anchored and unmoving and your spine erect, so that only the head moves.

Phase 3: Strength-Building Exercises

For maintaining and developing muscle tone and optimal levels of strength, do a few minutes of strength-building exercises following the flexibility phase of your warm-up. Determine early on what a reasonable number of each of these exercises is for you. It may be as few as 5 repetitions or as many as 50 . . . perhaps more. Once you've determined what you're capable of initially, try to gradually add more repetitions each week until you're doing the suggested number of minimum repetitions.

Trunk/Abdomen

1. Abdominal Curls
   Lie on your back with knees bent, feet on the floor, and arms folded across your chest. As you exhale, curl up in a slow, controlled fashion. There is no need to curl past 45 degrees. Repeat this exercise 20 times or until your abdominal muscles fatigue. Do not continue if you experience a burning sensation in the abdominal muscles.

Legs

2. Seated Leg Lifts
   Sit with your back straight and one leg extended in front of you. Bend the other leg, draw the knee up close to your chest, and place the foot on the floor. While keeping your trunk anchored and unmoving, lift the extended leg 3 to 12 inches off the floor and hold it for a count of 5. Lower the leg, and then repeat the exercise 4 more times for a total of 5 repetitions.

Repeat the exercise with the other leg extended. Make sure that you're not holding your breath as you do this exercise. Exhale as you lift, and then continue regular breathing as you slowly count to 5.

Shoulders/Arms/Hands

3. Push-Ups
   There is simply no better calisthenic for building upper-body strength than the standard push-up. If you're unable to do one of these, start out by doing the variation described following the description of the Standard Push-Up.

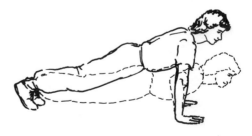

Standard: Keep your feet together, hands about shoulder-width apart, your back absolutely straight, and eyes trained straight ahead. Keep your elbows in by your sides and lower your trunk to a point about 3 inches from the floor. Then push yourself away and back to the preparatory position. As you do these, be sure to inhale as you lower yourself, and then exhale as you push up. Avoid a sagging midsection because this can put considerable pressure on your lower back. Work your way up to 10 repetitions or more.

Variation: If you're unable to do one standard push-up, try this variation. It involves doing essentially the same as described earlier for the standard push-up, except that you'll be pressing away from a wall or counter rather than the floor.

Position your feet about 3 feet from the wall or ledge, and place your hands on the wall at approximately shoulder height. Then let your upper body drop slowly forward. When your chest is about 3 inches from the surface, push away. This will be considerably easier than doing floor push-ups, and still helps you to build strength in your upper body.

When you can do 25 of these, try the standard push-up again. Prepare yourself for a dramatic drop in the number of repetitions compared to what you can do against the wall, but you'll probably be able to do at least a few floor push-ups now. That's a good start. Over a period of time, work your way up to 10 standard push-ups.

Phase 4: Cool-Down

At the close of your workout, while your muscles are warm, repeat the seven flexibility exercises from Phase 2.

Each of us may at some time face a violent or potentially violent person. It could happen in your home and involve someone you know, and perhaps even love. It may occur at work with a co-worker or client or patient. It may take place on the street and involve a total stranger. Increasing your awareness about the nature, typical circumstances, and dynamics of various forms of assaultive or threatening behavior can help you respond effectively should a threat arise.

HOW DO YOU BECOME MORE AWARE?

By examining data gathered by various governmental agencies and private researchers, you can develop a more thorough understanding of two broad categories of violent crime, assault and sexual assault. *Assault* is the more general category, encompassing all manner of aggressive behavior directed toward either male or female, in a wide variety of circumstances. *Sexual assault* refers to that particular form of violence where power, anger, and sexuality meet. Sexual assault is more often, though not exclusively, directed at females.

Data on assault help reveal when one is most at risk, what behaviors and strategies may reduce vulnerability, and which responses are most effective in deterring assailants when all efforts at avoidance fail.

ASSAULT

According to 1987 U.S. Department of Justice statistics, "five out of six people will be the victims of violent crimes, either attempted or completed, at least once during their lives" (Koppel, 1987, p. 3). Most of these will be *simple assaults*, in which less-than-serious bodily injury is intended and no weapon is used. *Aggravated assault*, in which serious bodily injury is intended and a weapon is

used, is less common. The vast majority of assaults, both simple and aggravated, involve one attacker and one intended victim.

Location and Time of Assault

Over half of assaults occur at night, most in the general vicinity of the victim's home. In fact, an attack involving an acquaintance or a relative is most likely to occur in or very near the home. An assault by a stranger is more likely to occur on the street. And as you might expect, those of us living in cities are generally at greater risk of assault than suburban or rural dwellers, according to a 1988 government report (United States Department of Justice, 1988).

Victims of Assault

It's difficult to tell who might be a "typical" or likely victim, given that the available data are frequently insufficient and misleading. For instance, victimization studies compiled by government agencies are based only on assaults reported to authorities. The 1988 U.S. Department of Justice report estimated that these reported assaults account for less than half the number that actually occur. And experts on family violence, such as domestic and child assault, suggest that more of those crimes go unreported.

It is in this area of family violence that women and children are at greatest risk and make up the majority of victims. The 1980 research of Straus, Gelles, and Steinmetz (cited in U.S. Department of Justice, 1988) suggests that between 1.8 and 5.7 million couples experience violence annually. And Finkelhor (1979) found that 19 percent of females and 9 percent of males are sexually abused as children.

Outside of family violence, men are more often the victims of assault. The 1988 U.S.

Department of Justice report indicated that young males have the highest violent victimization rate and elderly females the lowest. Blacks and other minorities also have higher victimization rates than whites relative to overall national patterns.

Occupation is also related to victimization. Harlow (1989) reports that service workers had twice the injury rate from violent victimization than that of all employed persons. Specific higher-risk occupations included police officers, recreation workers, bartenders, and taxi drivers. Among those with the lowest rates were farmers.

Assailants

Official records and victim surveys are two primary sources of information about who commits violent crime. Once again, these records can only provide information about those crimes and criminals that are brought to the attention of authorities. Because child abuse and spouse battering are grossly underreported, the assailant in these highly prevalent crimes is underrepresented in most official profiles of "typical assailants." Even so, the 1988 U.S. Department of Justice report cites independent research indicating that 90 percent of victimizers in child and domestic abuse cases are males who come from all socioeconomic, ethnic, and racial groupings.

It has also been argued that persons belonging to certain population sectors are overrepresented. For example, some critics have charged that because proportionally more young males and blacks are arrested and imprisoned than females or whites, the public often perceives them as comprising the bulk of assailants.

It's important to bear all of this in mind when examining data such as the following. These generalizations developed by the 1988 U.S. Department of Justice report suggest that persons arrested for assault are most likely to be

- between 18 and 34,
- male,
- known to the victim at least half the time,

- involved in use of alcohol just prior to commission of the assault, and
- white, although "blacks are perceived to be offenders in numbers disproportionate to their share of the population" (p. 41).

SEXUAL ASSAULT

Sexual assault is thought to be one of the most frequently committed crimes of violence in the U.S. Various studies have conservatively estimated that somewhere between 1 out of 3 and 1 out of 5 women over the age of 12 will be faced with rape or attempted rape at some time (see Johnson, 1989). Despite its frequency, sexual assault has long been surrounded by popular misconceptions, many of which place blame on the victims.

Victims

Women of all socioeconomic and ethnic backgrounds, ages, sizes, shapes, and levels of fitness have been victims of sexual assault. Two key factors in the selection of potential victims are vulnerability and accessibility. Despite some commonly held beliefs, "provocative" or "seductive" dress or behavior are *not* key factors. In fact, one study, reported in Rodabaugh and Austin (1981), found that less than 4 percent of sexual assaults involved "precipitative behavior" on the part of the victim.

Another popular misconception is that women frequently bring false charges of rape for revenge or other reasons. In fact, researchers have found that this occurs no more often than is the case with any other felony—that is, less than 2 percent of the time. Indeed, rape is considered to be one of the most *underreported* of violent crimes, with an optimistically estimated 10 to 30 percent being reported (Borgida & Brekke, 1985).

Knight, Rosenberg, and Schneider (1985) found that only about 10 percent of reported rapes result in arrests. Further, Rodabaugh and Austin found that only 2 percent result in convictions. This extremely low rate of arrest and conviction may explain the reluctance of victims to submit themselves to the often grueling process of police investigation and prosecution.

Assailants

Research conducted over the last 15 years has also laid to rest a number of misconceptions about assailants. Assailants, like their victims, come from all socioeconomic, ethnic, and racial backgrounds, and they also vary in age and physical condition. Because assailants select victims who are most accessible to them, both usually belong to the same socioeconomic grouping and race, according to Menachim Amir in his now classic *Patterns in Forcible Rape* (1971).

In addition, rapists are not easily distinguishable on the basis of physical or psychological characteristics from other men. Rodabaugh and Austin (1981) write,

Studies have shown that an overwhelming majority of rapists do not differ significantly from the norm in their physical or psychological characteristics, except for a tendency to be more likely to express hostility and frustration. In fact, rapists may be young, attractive, and personable. Many rapes begin with an ordinary social contact in which the victim is lulled into a sense of complacency and trust in the attacker. (p. 23)

Often this complacency and trust stem from a previous casual or even intimate relationship with the assailant. Many studies have found that over half of all sexual assaults involve assailants who are known to the victims, most often described as acquaintances.

A *Ms.* magazine study (Koss, 1985) found that of the 25 percent of women in college who have been raped, 90 percent knew their attackers. Furthermore, 47 percent of these rapes were committed by first or casual dates, or by romantic acquaintances.

And contrary to the stereotype that assumes that assaults occur mostly in dark alleys and parking lots, statistics indicate that between one third and two thirds of all rapes occur in the victim's home or another private residence (Rodabaugh & Austin, 1981).

Researchers have found that most assaults are planned in advance. Amir (1971) found that 71 percent of rapes he studied involved premeditation. Preplanning was even more likely in pair rapes (two assailants and one victim) and gang rapes (three or more assailants and one victim).

We look to Dr. Nicholas Groth, a specialist in treating sex offenders, to help us understand the assailant's motivation. Groth and Birnbaum (1979) found that there are three primary components in sexual assault—power, anger, and sexuality. They write

Moreover, in our experience, we find that either anger or power is the dominant component and that rape, rather than being primarily an expression of sexual desire, is, in fact, the use of sexuality to express these issues of power and anger. (p. 13)

Groth and Birnbaum describe three patterns of sexual assault—power rape, anger rape, and sadistic rape. They identify power rape, which accounts for over 55 percent of the cases studied, as the most common pattern. In these cases, the assailant is motivated primarily by a desire for mastery and conquest. The assailant achieves his goal of power and control by intimidating the victim with threats, physical aggression, or the display of a weapon. This type of assailant uses only the degree of force necessary to overcome the victim's resistance.

Anger rape is the next most common pattern and accounts for 40 percent of those cases studied by Groth and Birnbaum. These assaults are characterized by a great deal of anger and rage, directed both verbally and physically at the victim. These cases involve "far more force . . . than would be necessary if the intent were simply to overpower the victim" (p. 13). Groth and Birnbaum suggest that 40 percent may be an overestimation of anger rapes. Because of the greater violence and abuse inflicted, they suspect that this group is more often convicted and consequently overrepresented in their sample consisting entirely of convicted rapists. Groth and Birnbaum further suggest that "power rapists" are underrepresented in their sample and may account for a larger proportion of rapists in general.

The third pattern, accounting for about 5 percent of Groth and Birnbaum's sample, is sadistic rape. In these rapes, "aggression itself becomes eroticized" (p. 44). Sadistic rape is very often bizarre and ritualistic, and may involve bondage and torture.

In all three of these distinctive patterns of sexual assault, Groth and Birnbaum found greater preoccupation on the part of assailants with "status, hostility, control, and dominance than with sensual pleasure or sexual satisfaction" (p.11).

Stages of Sexual Assault

Various researchers have found that there are at least three distinct stages in sexual assault, beginning with *selection of a victim*. According to the Queen's Bench Foundation's Project Rape Response (U.S. Department of Justice, 1976), "Assailants engaged in a selection process, often eliminating some women until they found a suitable victim. . . . The majority of offenders selected women whom they perceived as available and/or vulnerable" (p. 2).

Selection is often followed by a *testing stage*. In this stage, the assailant approaches and engages a potential victim in some sort of interaction, often characterized by the Queen's Bench report as a "typically friendly and impersonal" conversation (p. 2). This period of interaction, varying from a few seconds to hours, "seems to be a means for the offender to assess the victim and subtly assert his control, setting the process of dominance into motion" (p. 2). According to Dr. James Selkin (1975) and others who have written of this sequence of events, threats and intimidation are common during this stage as assailants test their victims for compliance and submissiveness.

Unless the process of dominance described above is interrupted, the assault usually escalates to a third stage, that of *physical aggression*.

Resistance

The most effective way of addressing the question of resistance is in terms of the three stages just outlined. You'll certainly want to resist being selected as a victim, and it appears that the best way to do this is to project an unvictimlike, confident, and vigilant demeanor. According to the Queen's Bench report (U.S. Department of Justice, 1976), "Physical appearance or assertive body language were factors which led to elimination of prospective victims" (p. 2).

During the testing stage, firm verbal and psychological resistance appears to be effective in suggesting to a would-be assailant that you're lousy victim material. The Queen's Bench report found that women who deterred attackers, in contrast with those who were assaulted, "tended to be somewhat more suspicious and more often responded in a hostile or rude manner prior to the signal of attack" (p. 3).

Once a situation reaches the point of physical aggression, and even before, the decision regarding *how* or even *whether* to resist can only be made by the intended victim. As a potential victim, you're the only person who knows the specific situational factors involved, as well as the particular strengths and skills you bring to the situation, and only you can weigh risks involved in various possible responses, make a choice, and act on it.

It's also important to point out that a solid body of research conducted over the past 15 years indicates that immediate and firm resistance is a key factor in deterring unarmed attacks. These studies suggest that vigorous physical and verbal resistance such as running, shouting, and striking frequently results in interrupted attacks. In contrast, passive resistance, consisting of begging, pleading, or verbal stalling, does not typically deter attacks.

Several studies suggest that a willingness to use more than one type of resistance measure was effective in deterring assailants. In fact, the Queen's Bench study invited comments from convicted sex offenders who believed "they would have been deterred if the victim had resisted more vigorously both physically and verbally" (p. 4). The offenders advised "assertive verbal objection, self-defense techniques, and/or screaming or running" (p. 4). Regarding prevention of assault, the Queen's Bench study summed it up best:

> Successful resistance is not so much a matter of using the "best" method as it is one of awareness and preparedness: For women to deter assault they must be alert and suspicious, and not be overwhelmed by fear and panic. They must focus on ways to get out of the situation, be determined not to be raped, be willing to risk and experience pain or injury, and present a firm resistance. (p. 5)

Awareness Drills

1. Self-Study of Precautionary Measures

Conduct a self-study to identify areas of your life where you can reduce your vulnerability and accessibility to an assailant. Weigh each precaution carefully and decide whether it is appropriate and feasible for you. Blend those that you select into your life patterns so that they become routine. Throughout this process, keep in mind that your goal is not to limit your life, but rather to make it more secure.

Self-Study of Precautions

Rate your typical response in the following situations. The higher the response number, the more the item is true.

a. In the Street

1. Do you generally walk assertively? Do you look confident, vigilant, unafraid, and as if you know where you are going?

    (Value: 0-2 points) _____

2. Is this still true when you feel ill, preoccupied, or are in an unfamiliar area?

    (Value: 0-2 points) _____

3. Do you walk on the outside of a sidewalk, away from doorways and shrubs?

    (Value: 1 point) _____

4. Do you keep your purse or briefcase close to you to prevent someone from grabbing it?

    (Value: 1 point) _____

5. Do you wear comfortable clothing that will allow you to run when you know you'll be out walking?

    (Value: 0-2 points) _____

6. Do you think through the routes you frequently walk? (Are you aware of the location of public or all-night places? friends' homes? police or fire stations? telephones? least safe points along your route?)

(Value: 1-2 points) _____

7. Do you vary your usual route in order to be less predictable?

(Value: 1 point) _____

Maximum Point Value for Precautions Taken in the Street .... 11 _____

b. In Your Home

1. Do you have solid dead bolt locks on your doors?

(Value: 2 points) _____

2. Do you have a chain lock in order to identify callers before completely opening your door?

(Value: 1 point) _____

3. Do you have a wide-angle peephole in your door?

(Value: 1 point) _____

4. Do you have escape routes planned from various spots in your home in the event that you need to get out fast?

(Value: 1 point) _____

5. If you live alone, do you list only the initial of your first name and leave your address out of the telephone directory?

(Value: 0-2 points) _____

6. Do you have effective locks or bar braces on your sliding doors and windows?

(Value: 2 points) _____

7. Do you avoid hiding house keys outside in predictable hiding places, such as under porch ornaments, above the door, or under the door mat?

(Value: 1 point) _____

8. Do you keep one or more of these by your bed: flashlight, whistle or shriek alarm, telephone?

(Value: 0-3 points) _____

Maximum Point Value for Precautions Taken in Your Home .... 13 _____

c. In Your Car

1. Do you keep the following items in your vehicle: flare, white rag, maps, first aid kit, flashlight, tool kit, proper change for a phone call, spare tire/jack?

(Value: 1/2 point each) _____

2. Do you keep car doors locked while driving?

(Value: 1 point) _____

3. Do you check the backseat of your car before getting in?

(Value: 1 point) _____

4. When driving in unfamiliar neighborhoods, do you make sure you have clear directions? Do you have a reliable vehicle?

(Value: 2 points) _____

Maximum Point Value for Precautions Taken in Your Car............................8 _____

Success Goals =

a. In the Street (80 percent of maximum possible points or 9 points)

b. In Your Home (80 percent of maximum possible points or 10 points)

c. In Your Car (80 percent of maximum possible points or 6 points)

d. Total Points for Precautionary Measures (80 percent of maximum possible or 26 points)

Your Score =

a. (#)_____ points/In the Street

b. (#)_____ points/In Your Home

c. (#)_____ points/In Your Car

d. (#)_____ total points for Precautionary Measures

2. Special Projects*

Each of the following projects is intended to deepen your awareness of the social context of violence and aggression. Select one or more of these to do, as time and interest allow. Give yourself 10 points for each completed project.

A. Critique a newspaper article or a news report on a sexual assault from radio or television. Note the degree to which the report
   - supports or challenges misconceptions,
   - instills fear or encourages action,
   - provides accurate information and analysis, and
   - provides useful information that will help you improve your individual or your community's safety.

B. Imagine that the world is completely at peace and that people no longer harm or rob each other. Describe something you would do if you didn't have to fear or adapt to danger from other people.

---

*Projects A and B are based on the work of San Francisco-based self-defense instructor Nina Smith.

C. It has been suggested that North Americans have a great tolerance for violence and aggression as depicted in forms of popular culture such as movies, television, books, and games. From these general areas of popular culture, choose a specific focus, for example, Saturday morning television cartoons, 5 days of prime-time television on a major network, or three top-grossing movies of the preceding year. Keep a record of the number of incidences of aggression or violence. Once again, note whether misconceptions of violence are challenged or reinforced. Also, note patterns in the depiction of gender, class, race, and age of assailants and victims.

D. Find information on crime prevention services and services to victims of violence in your community. Possible sources include rape crisis centers, victim assistance and compensation programs, domestic violence shelters, child abuse prevention centers, and neighborhood watch organizations. Discuss the ways in which individuals can work together to improve the safety and security of their neighborhoods and communities.

Success Goal = 10 points minimum (40 possible)

Your Score = (#)_____ project points

Step 2 Assessment

The second of the three A's is Assessment. As stated earlier, assessment refers to the process of quickly and accurately evaluating a specific situation in which you feel at risk. Proper assessment of a potentially violent situation requires presence of mind and solid observational and perceptual skills.

WHY IS ASSESSMENT IMPORTANT?

Skillful and rapid assessment of a potentially dangerous situation is necessary in order to select effective and appropriate strategies for preventing violence. We rely on our observational skills to gather information that is as accurate and complete as possible in order to make the best possible choices in threatening circumstances.

HOW DO YOU ASSESS A SITUATION?

In assessing a situation, it's important to take note of *where* you are and *who* is involved. This means gathering information about (a) the immediate environment, (b) the threatening individual, and (c) yourself.

The Environment

In any potentially dangerous situation, you'll want to take in as much information as possible about your surroundings. Ask yourself what sort of violence you might expect in this environment: robbery, sexual assault, general assault. It's especially important to note the following:

- *All possible avenues of escape.* This includes doors and windows, if you are indoors. If outdoors, note where there are likely to be more people, better lit areas, help, and safety.
- *Number, proximity, and identity of other people nearby.* Determine whether others

nearby are a source of help, or whether they represent an additional threat.
- *Large objects that can serve as barriers.* You may need to position yourself behind a desk, large couch, counter, car, bed, or other obstacle.
- *Smaller objects you can pick up and use as shields or as "weapons of opportunity" if the need arises.* You may have to protect yourself with your briefcase, purse, walking stick or cane, a sofa cushion, a pot or pan, a bathroom scale, a stick, a small chair, an end table, and so on. People have scooped up handfuls of dirt, sand, gravel, or pocket change to fling at assailants in order to create an opportunity to get away.
- *Time of day.* How many people are out and about, within range to see or hear what's going on?
- *Evidence of substance abuse, such as bottles and drug paraphernalia.* This cues you to consider the possibility of the potential assailant's being intoxicated or under the influence of drugs.

The Threatening Individual

Look carefully at this person. Try to pick up the entire message being conveyed. Attend to both verbal and nonverbal cues, and note whether these are in agreement. Put your thoughts, feelings, and biases on hold temporarily while you take in as much information as possible and assess his or her frame of mind and intentions. Look for anything that tells you what to expect from the potential attacker. Things you'll need to observe about a threatening person include these:

- *Identity.* Do you know this person? If so, what do you know about him or her?
- *Positioning and proximity to you.* How close to you is the person? Is he or she blocking your avenue of escape?

- *Size, strength, and conditioning.*
- *Demeanor, stance, and posture.* Is his or her demeanor threatening? Skittish or fidgety? Undecided? Is she or he moving toward you? Is it an angry demeanor? Are shoulders pushed forward aggressively, hands and jaws clenched, coloring flushed, lips tight, and neck rigid? Is the individual displaying signs of fear or nervousness, such as shallow breathing, increased blinking, working of the jaw, frequent swallowing, licking of the lips, compulsive jerking of the hands, or pallor?
- *Emotional state.* Does this person seem fearful or angry? (Note behavior clusters associated with these two states of mind as indicated earlier.) Does she or he seem frustrated, panicky, confused, irrational, paranoid, under the influence of drugs or alcohol?
- *Gait.* Is it lurching or unsteady? Is movement purposeful?
- *Gestures.* Are movements wild, jerky, and agitated? Do you notice extraneous shifting and twitching? Or is the person absolutely still and watchful?
- *Clothes.* What, if anything, does this person's clothing tell you about him or her?
- *What he or she is saying, and how.* Is the voice loud and belligerent? Is the throat tight and the voice strained? Are words slurred?
- *Possession of actual weapons or availability of makeshift weapons.*

You

An accurate sense of your own capabilities is a critical part of any assessment. Two different people faced with identical environments and threatening individuals will very likely select different responses, based on their different strengths, skills, and states of mind.

Strengths. Are you fleet of foot, or slow-moving? Are you relatively strong, or do you lack muscular strength? Can you shout loudly to attract attention, or is your voice faint? Are you capable of maintaining presence of mind in emergencies, including the emergency of assault?

Skills. Are you trained in self-defense or martial arts? Are you skillful at verbally defusing potentially dangerous encounters?

Feeling state. Are you able to maintain calm and to think clearly about options and possible outcomes? Do your instincts tell you to break and run as fast and as soon as you can?

Assessment skills improve with practice. Take stock now, under nonstressful circumstances, of your ability to assess environments, read people, and control your own feeling state. Consider how much more challenging this would be in a highly charged and dangerous situation. The following drills can help you improve the observational and perceptual skills so critical to an accurate and thorough assessment of volatile situations.

Assessment Drills

1. Environment Assessment Drill

This drill is intended to give new meaning to the phrase *environmental awareness*. Plan a tour of 10 different sites within close proximity of each other. Include several rooms in your home or apartment, at least two other indoor sites (e.g., your office or work environment, lobbies, or hallways) and a few outdoor areas. Once positioned at each site, give yourself 10 seconds to take in as much information about the setting as possible. Keep in mind those factors listed previously under "The Environment."

Success Goal = Identification of (a) avenues of escape, (b) barriers, (c) shields and weapons of opportunity, and (d) other people at 8 out of 10 sites in no more than 10 seconds

Your Score = (#)_____ sites where key elements of environmental assessment were identified in 10 seconds or less

2. People-Reading Drill

The purpose of this drill is to become more aware of how you identify emotional states in others and, in particular, those emotional states associated with violence and aggression.

We read people constantly in social situations, usually quite casually and without much awareness of what we're doing. In this drill, you'll identify the behavioral cues and body language that tell you what another person is feeling. As you observe, ask yourself constantly, "*How do I know that this person is angry/confused/panicky/joyful/bored?*"

Spend 30 minutes in a public place where you're likely to see some intense displays of emotion. This might be at a football game or boxing match, a hospital emergency room, or a large airport. If you feel uncomfortable observing people in this way, select a highly dramatic film to watch. From a distance, try to read people's emotional states by their posture, demeanor, movements, gestures, and expressions. Pay special attention to the body language that generally accompanies anger, frustration, and fear.

Keep in mind, of course, that there are many shades of expression and mixtures of emotion that make identification of feeling states imprecise. Discuss your observations with your teacher or others in your class.

Success Goal = 30 minutes of people-reading

Your Score = _____ Project completed (yes? or no?)

3. Self-Assessment Drill

Conduct an inventory of skills, strengths, and personal resources you can depend on when facing volatile or threatening situations. As you complete the inventory below, recall your responses in other types of emergencies. Think about ways you've used these strengths and skills in the past, and how you might use them to best advantage in potential assaultive situations. Once you've completed the inventory, consider which of these you can improve and how you might do this. Identify at least five areas of possible improvement.

Inventory of Skills/Strengths

Rate the following skills/strengths/personal resources on a scale of 1 to 5, with 1 indicating *none or little* and 5 indicating *a great deal*. Circle the number that most closely reflects your ability.

Physical Skills

Speed, can run/move fast	1	2	3	4	5
Endurance, can run far/move continuously	1	2	3	4	5

Muscular strength (lower body)	1	2	3	4	5
Muscular strength (upper body)	1	2	3	4	5
Balance	1	2	3	4	5
Imposing size	1	2	3	4	5
Self-confident, erect posture	1	2	3	4	5
Assertive body language (make and maintain eye contact, feet shoulder-width apart, weight evenly distributed, take up full space, relaxed and erect posture)	1	2	3	4	5
Other _____	1	2	3	4	5

Mental and Emotional Strengths/Skills

Habits/routines that reflect caution and concern with safety	1	2	3	4	5
Ability to project a vigilant and unvictimlike persona	1	2	3	4	5
Observant, quick to identify dangerous people and situations	1	2	3	4	5
Capacity for verbal assertiveness	1	2	3	4	5
Presence of mind in emergencies	1	2	3	4	5
Self-assurance and self-confidence	1	2	3	4	5
Ability to maintain calm, resistance to panic	1	2	3	4	5
Courage in the face of threat (or at least bravado)	1	2	3	4	5
Flexibility to adjust to a rapidly changing scene	1	2	3	4	5
Capable of positive self-talk in a threatening situation	1	2	3	4	5
Determination, ability to maintain commitment to a goal	1	2	3	4	5
Resilience, ability to recover, and fight back in different ways, perhaps in court later	1	2	3	4	5
Capacity for aggressive physical action	1	2	3	4	5
Other _____	1	2	3	4	5

Possible Areas of Improvement

1.
2.
3.
4.
5.

Success Goals =

a. Complete inventory of skills and strengths useful in a potential assaultive situation

b. Identification of 5 areas of potential improvement

Your Score =

a. _____ Inventory completed (yes? or no?)

b. _____ 5 areas identified (yes? or no?)

Step 3   Action

In this step, the three action strategies of Immediate Retreat, De-Escalation, and Assertiveness/Confrontation will be explored—prior to self-defense. After two decades of teaching self-defense and hearing literally hundreds of stories from people who have successfully defended themselves, I've come to believe that the most effective resistance takes place *before* a situation becomes physically violent.

The Action we take in a potentially assaultive situation is based on the interplay between our general knowledge and experience of interpersonal aggression (Awareness) and our rapid evaluation of an immediately threatening situation (Assessment). Action is also based on an understanding of strategies for defense and their possible outcomes.

In many potentially assaultive situations, your choice may be to retreat immediately. In other situations, you may attempt verbal and psychological tactics to discourage a threatening individual from becoming physically aggressive by using either de-escalation or assertiveness/confrontation skills, which are useful in different contexts.

Finally, you may be forced to physically defend yourself. This may follow one of the other three action strategies, or it may, of necessity, be your first response.

WHY IS IMMEDIATE RETREAT AN IMPORTANT OPTION?

Immediate retreat, as a response to a potentially assaultive situation, provides the best possible chance of avoiding injury or harm in most cases. Most people will consider this option before any other, unless retreat would place them or another person at even greater risk. In fact, most states have laws requiring retreat from potential violence whenever possible. People attacked in their homes and certain law enforcement personnel are exempt from this legal requirement to retreat.

HOW DO I RETREAT?

How you retreat will depend on the circumstances. In some cases, retreat may take the form of a high-speed sprint in the direction that you perceive to be the safest. For instance, imagine you're a man walking home from the library quite late in the evening. As you're walking through a fairly desolate neighborhood, you notice someone following you. You're aware of this person getting closer to you, and realize at the same time that she or he is carrying what looks like a knife. You shout to attract attention and run as fast as possible toward an all-night restaurant a quarter of a block away.

Or your retreat may be more subtle as in the following Bus Stop Scene.

Bus Stop Scene

Imagine you're a woman waiting for a bus late one afternoon in a relatively busy section of town. A man standing nearby, also presumably waiting for a bus, engages you in conversation. He asks a number of casual questions, but then begins to ask questions about where and with whom you live. As his questions take a more personal turn, you notice that he's moved disconcertingly close to you. His questions and behavior become increasingly intrusive and your uneasiness grows.

In this situation, you're unlikely to break into a full-speed dash to safety. But you'll probably terminate the conversation abruptly and walk briskly in the direction of possible assistance. While walking away, you look pointedly over your shoulder to make sure that you are not being followed.

Both of these responses constitute immediate retreat, because both involve making a preemptive escape from a potentially dangerous situation and moving toward safety as quickly as circumstances warrant.

DE-ESCALATION

De-escalation, called *soft self-defense*, consists of verbal, psychological, and nonverbal techniques for defusing potentially dangerous situations. The de-escalation strategies and techniques presented here are eclectic, and have been culled from writings on this topic from fields such as criminal justice, communication, psychology, crisis management, and conflict resolution. De-escalation tactics are increasingly emphasized in self-defense training as a strategy for postponing physical aggression. You should know, however, that this component of training is new and still very experimental.

The goal of de-escalation is to build rapid rapport and a sense of connectedness with an agitated person in order to reduce the likelihood of escalation to physical violence. This requires that the defender control his or her own emotional response to threat in order to deal with someone already close to losing control.

These are not techniques for controlling another person. In fact, attempting to do this can be counterproductive. Controlling *yourself* and controlling *communication* enable you to reverse the escalating dynamics of a situation.

WHY ARE DE-ESCALATION SKILLS IMPORTANT?

De-escalation skills are useful in dealing with people who are highly agitated, frustrated, angry, fearful, or intoxicated. These may be ordinarily peaceful individuals who are responding to unusual or extreme circumstances. Or they may be persons who generally have volatile and disruptive personalities. (Note: These skills are *not* appropriate for use with potential sexual assailants, given the distinct psychodynamics of sexual aggression. See the Assertiveness/Confrontation section later in this step.)

HOW DO I DE-ESCALATE?

There are both nonverbal and verbal principles involved in de-escalating a situation.

Nonverbal Principles of De-Escalation

It is said that nonverbal behaviors account for approximately 65 percent of communication. And of the remaining 35 percent, inflection, pitch, and loudness account for over 25 percent, while less than 7 percent has to do with choice of words. This should reassure those of you who find yourselves "at a loss for words" in dangerous situations.

There are three general principles governing our nonverbal response to a threatening and agitated individual. These are shown in Figure 3.1 and described in detail as follows.

Figure 3.1 Defensive posture used in de-escalation.

1. Project a Confident and Attentive Demeanor

a. Maintain eye contact. Avoid averting your gaze because this can be interpreted as an expression of fear, lack of interest or regard, or rejection. On the other hand, avoid staring, which can be threatening.
b. Assume a neutral facial expression. Looking bored or disapproving increases hostility, while a calm, attentive expression reduces hostility.
c. Keep a relaxed, alert posture. Keep your back straight, feet shoulder-width apart, and weight evenly distributed over both feet. Avoid slouching, folding, shrinking,

or aggressive stances. Monitor the tension in your shoulders, neck, hands, and face.

d. Minimize extraneous movement. Keep hand gestures to a minimum. Avoid sudden, jerky, or excessive movement. Stand still, rather than shifting from foot to foot or pacing.

2. Mirror Calm

Control your own level of arousal. High arousal states can interfere with mental and physical function—your own as well as that of the agitated individual. A low to moderate arousal level, on the other hand, keeps you alert and ready for necessary action. Two good techniques for controlling your own level of anxiety are the following:

a. Breath deeply and slowly from your diaphragm, and not your chest.

b. Use positive and affirming internal self-talk. Keep in mind that our thoughts about an event, person, or situation trigger particular emotional responses.

(the event) + (self-talk) = (feeling)

Many people either hold their breath or breathe very shallowly when faced with potential assault. People are also likely to be delivering undermining messages to themselves, such as ''I'm in real trouble now,'' or ''I'm probably going to be hurt badly.'' These reactions generally increase anxiety and fear, making it more difficult to think clearly about options and outcomes.

If you practice deep, slow breathing and positive self-talk regularly in response to any form of stress or anxiety, you'll be more likely to respond this way in dealing with the emergency of assault. These calming and centering behaviors can become a conditioned response to potential danger.

3. Position Yourself for Safety

a. Maintain a minimum distance of two arm's lengths between yourself and a potential assailant. By staying outside of this critical distance zone, you remain slightly out of range of strikes, grabs, and sudden lunges.

b. Angle your body approximately 45 degrees. By angling your body, you present fewer vulnerable areas of your body that could serve as targets for a physical attack. This also puts you in position to turn and run. (Note: Even as you keep your body angled, be sure to turn your face fully toward the person with whom you're talking.)

c. Keep your hands free and in front of your body. In this way, your hands are available for blocking if the need arises. Avoid folding your arms, jamming hands in your pockets, or clasping hands behind you.

d. Position yourself behind a barrier, if possible. Casually position yourself behind a sofa, desk, large chair, counter, table, or other large object when possible.

Sample Crisis Situation

Now, to better understand how you might apply these nonverbal principles, imagine for a moment that you're in the following threatening and potentially explosive situation.

Parking Lot Scene

You have a temporary job directing traffic in a makeshift parking lot set up to accommodate the large numbers of spectators attending a major sporting event on your campus. Given the makeshift nature of the lot, parking lanes and spaces are not clearly marked. To complicate things, there are large crowds of people on foot who have already parked their cars and are walking toward the stadium. The game has just begun and those people still having to park are anxious to do so. You approach a vehicle to direct the driver to a space he's unable to see clearly. Before you say anything, the man at the wheel begins to complain loudly and angrily about the wait. He berates the lack of adequate parking facilities and what he considers incompetent help. The other passengers are amused by the driver's anger and goad him on. Both driver and passengers appear to have been drinking.

You interrupt to direct the driver to the available parking space, not realizing that another attendant has just directed another car to the same spot. The angles of approach of the two vehicles are such that the drivers don't see one another until they collide. Both drivers jump out of their vehicles and are angrily shouting at each other as you dash up to them. The driver with whom you've just been talking suddenly turns on you, shouting and waving his arms threateningly.

In applying the nonverbal principles of de-escalation, you would first project confidence and attentiveness by looking this person directly in the eye, maintaining a neutral facial expression, minimizing gestures, and drawing yourself up full stature into a relaxed and erect posture. You would maintain your calm demeanor by breathing deeply and slowly and focusing on positive self-talk. You would also make sure that you are two arm's lengths from this person, and that your body is slightly angled. You would place your hands slightly in front of you, and, if possible to do so unobtrusively, you would keep the car door or fender between the two of you as you interacted.

Verbal Principles of De-Escalation

1. *Keep your voice calm, firm, and low, while speaking slowly and evenly.* Generally, a high-pitched voice and rapid speech tend to increase anxiety and agitation. Occasionally you may have to match the tone of voice of someone speaking loudly and rapidly in order to get their attention. Quickly lead them to a softer, slower pace.

2. *Listen actively.* Interact with this person. Use observational inquiries such as "You're pretty shaken up by this, aren't you?" Ask open-ended questions and encourage the person to talk by making comments such as "Yes, I see," "Uh huh," "Then what?" Note: It's not generally advisable to let someone vent and rage indefinitely. A recent study (Tavris, 1982) suggests that this behavior intensifies feelings of frustration and anger and may actually increase the likelihood of escalation to physical violence. Listen, gather information, ask questions, develop a rapport if possible, and begin to guide communication in a less volatile direction.

3. *Acknowledge the agitated person's feelings.* Reflecting someone's feelings back to them often lets them know that they are being heard. Some agitated people will have a difficult time problem-solving until their feelings are dealt with. You may need to say, "Look, I can see you're really angry about what's happened. But we need to make sure that everyone is okay."

4. *Communicate clearly.* Explain your intentions and convey your expectations clearly. You may need to repeat yourself until you are heard and understood. Use the person's name if you know it and make requests or suggestions simple and specific: "Mr. Brown . . . Mr. Brown . . . Stop shouting, please. I need you to see if everyone in your vehicle is okay."

5. *Avoid escalating behaviors.* Certain behaviors have been found to be inflammatory in dealing with highly agitated people:

   - Not listening to or ignoring the person
   - Making threats, such as "You take one step closer, mister, and you've had it!"
   - Unkind or hurtful remarks, for example, "Look, lamebrain, if you'd been watching where you were going. . . ."
   - Arguing, ("You're crazy. . . . It didn't happen that way at all!")
   - Commanding ("Shut up and sit down.")

- Shouting
- Invading personal space
- Using threatening gestures, such as finger-wagging and pointing
- Using obscenities
- Placing yourself in competition with the person ("Hey, you can't talk to me that way! Just who do you think you are?!")
- Taking a self-righteous attitude ("I would never behave so hysterically.")

6. *Use one or more of the defusing techniques outlined here, if appropriate for the situation:*

- Brainstorm solutions with this person for whatever is causing the agitation.
- Redirect the agitated person's attention. One technique that is sometimes effective involves directing this person's attention to something less disturbing or agitating. "What's the name of your insurance company, Mr. Brown? And who's your agent?" This makes Mr. Brown refocus momentarily on insurance details instead of his ire.
- Sit down with him or her. When people sit, all their major postural muscles relax. There is an automatic lowering of general arousal.
- Change the immediate environment. This is helpful when someone or something in the immediate environment is contributing to the person's agitation. ("Mr. Brown, come sit in this vehicle for a moment while we finish exchanging the necessary information.")
- Get to "Yes." A number of writers on negotiation, including Dr. Gordon Blush (1982), have pointed out the effectiveness of trying to find a point of agreement (usually nonsubstantive) in order to break down excessive opposition and unrelenting resistance. This is known as "building little agreements" to establish rapport and connectedness. You might try to connect with the other person by saying, "Mr. Brown, you want to get this taken care of as soon as possible so you can get on to the game, is that so?"

- Use humor—carefully. Humor is a powerful tension reliever and has significant physiological impact. It can reduce arousal by changing pulse rate, breathing patterns, and brain waves. On the other hand, if your humor is aggressive, insensitive, or easily misunderstood, the person may interpret it to mean that you're not taking his or her pain or anger seriously.
- Define behavioral limits. This involves setting limits or conditions for further interaction and is usually necessary when the agitated individual is becoming more aggressive—shouting into your face, for example, or pushing into your personal space. Here's an example of defining behavioral limits: "I'll continue discussing this with you, but first you'll have to lower your voice," or "We need to sit down in order to continue with this discussion."

This is far from an exhaustive list of defusing techniques for use with highly agitated people. You may have developed techniques of your own that are useful in dealing with particular populations or groups. What is important is that you constantly monitor the impact of your own behaviors and statements on the arousal level of a potentially explosive person throughout your interaction. Remember that building rapport requires that you open yourself to this other person, despite her or his extreme agitation. Finally, keep in mind that you're most likely to prevent a volatile situation from becoming violent by controlling your own anxiety, fear, or even anger, and by controlling communication.

De-Escalation Drills

1. Nonverbal Principles Practice Drill

The purpose of this drill is to sharpen awareness of those behaviors that are part of nonverbal communication.

Stand facing a practice partner and pretend that she or he is a highly agitated, potentially explosive person. Incorporate as many of the suggestions regarding nonverbal behavior as you remember. Ask a third person to check each of the nonverbal behaviors as you demonstrate it. Give yourself 1 point for each behavior that is checked.

Take note of the ease or difficulty you have with applying these suggestions. For instance, many people have a difficult time maintaining the required distance. Because the conversational range in North America is about one arm's length, some people automatically seek out that distance, even in situations where doing so increases risk. A distance of two arm's lengths provides an important safety buffer.

Success Goal = 7 of 10 possible checks for correctly demonstrating the following nonverbal behaviors

Assume a confident and vigilant demeanor
Eyes on other person's eyes? _____
Facial expression neutral? _____
Posture relaxed and alert? _____
Movement minimized? _____

Mirror calm
Breathing deeply and slowly? _____
Using positive self-talk? _____

Position yourself for safety
Distance of two arm's lengths? _____
Body angled at 45 degrees? _____
Hands free and in front of body? _____
Using available barriers? _____

Your Score = (#)_____ behaviors correctly demonstrated

2. Self-Monitoring Drill

The purpose of this drill is to increase awareness of your ability to maintain a calm and centered presence in stressful or emergency circumstances. Over a period of about 2 weeks, note how you respond to specific threatening or stressful incidents. Do not include chronic or long-standing stress-inducing situations. Rather, limit your monitoring to single, specific events, such as a particularly unpleasant phone call, giving a speech, or taking a test. Note your breathing patterns (Do you hold your breath? take shallow breaths?) and self-talk (affirming? or undermining?).

Once you've determined your general patterns, experiment with consciously slowing and deepening your breathing in response to stress or threats. Also, come up with some simple, affirming statements to use in these situations, such as ''I can handle this situation'' or ''I have the skills to deal with this.''

Success Goal = List the 3 most stressful situations encountered during the past 2 weeks, include your immediate self-thoughts, and change them to affirmations, as appropriate

Your Score =

Stressful situation	Undermining self-talk	Affirming self-talk
1.		
2.		
3.		

3. Role-Playing/The Lost Project Report

This drill provides an opportunity to practice de-escalation skills in a simulated situation. You'll be assisted in this role-playing by two other people. One of them will pretend to be a highly agitated individual. The other will be an observer whose task is to watch your efforts to de-escalate the agitated person and then give you feedback on your application of the verbal and nonverbal principles.

Once the role-playing begins, both the ''agitated person'' and the ''de-escalator'' should remain in character for 1 minute. The agitated person should respond realistically to the de-escalator's efforts by calming down or becoming more upset, depending on whether she or he finds the de-escalator's behaviors calming or inflammatory, respectively. Throughout the role-playing, the observer stands a few feet away, taking note of posture, stance, positioning, demeanor, voice tone, and use of either escalating or defusing techniques.

Stop the role-playing after 1 minute. At this point, observers share their observations. Role players then analyze the dynamics of the interaction, noting when they felt the tension lessening or increasing and discussing possible reasons for this. The role-playing situation follows.

Lost Project Report

The agitated person has come into an office shared with the de-escalator. The former begins to look for a project report left on a worktable the night before. This project is to be turned in to a supervisor within half an hour. Failure to do so may result in severe sanctions for the agitated person, who already has been placed on probationary status for failure to complete work assignments in a timely manner.

The worktable is a mess, due in large part to the de-escalator's sloppy work habits. The project report—finished only the night before after considerable effort—can't be found. The agitated person has a number of other problems in his or her life at the moment. These other problems (severe and complicated family problems, illness, other deadlines) have created an extraordinary level of stress. (Note: Dr. Gordon Blush (1982) has found that people generally go through a process of accumulating grievances before they allow themselves to act violently. Violence frequently follows what is perceived to be the last straw.)

The agitated person becomes increasingly angry, frustrated, and distraught at not being able to find the project report. You, the sloppy office mate, walk in to face this person.

Success Goal = Minimum of 12 out of 21 possible points

Nonverbal Behaviors (*Gain 1 point each*)

Assume a confident and vigilant demeanor
Eyes on other person's eyes? _____
Facial expression neutral? _____
Posture relaxed and alert? _____
Movement minimized? _____

Mirror calm
Breathing deeply and slowly? _____
Using positive self-talk? _____

Position yourself for safety
Distance of two arm's lengths? _____
Body angled at 45 degrees? _____
Hands free and in front of body? _____
Using available barriers? _____

Verbal Behaviors (*Gain 1 point each*)

Using calm, controlled voice? _____
Active listening? _____
Acknowledging feelings? _____
Clear communication? _____
Use of defusing techniques:

- Brainstorming solutions? _____
- Redirecting? _____
- Person sitting down? _____
- Changing immediate environment? _____
- Getting to "yes" agreement? _____
- Using humor effectively? _____
- Defining behavioral limits? _____

Escalating Behaviors (*Lose 1 point each*)

- Not listening to or ignoring the person? _____
- Threatening? _____
- Making unkind or hurtful remarks? _____
- Arguing? _____
- Commanding? _____
- Shouting? _____
- Invading space? _____
- Using threatening gestures? _____
- Using obscenities? _____
- Competing? _____
- Sounding self-righteous? _____

Your Score = (#) _____ nonverbal points + (#) _____ verbal points − (#) _____ escalating behaviors = (#) _____ total points

ASSERTIVENESS/CONFRONTATION SKILLS

Assertiveness/Confrontation refers to verbal and psychological skills useful in dealing with a sexual assailant motivated by a desire for dominance and control. These techniques are most effective when used during the testing stage of an assault. You may recall from our discussion in the "Awareness" section that this stage is characterized by efforts on the part of the assailant to establish the process of dominance through the use of verbal threat and negotiation. This state usually precedes physical force and aggression.

Confrontation at this stage represents a potential victim's firm and direct refusal to comply with behaviors that an assailant expects from a typical victim.

WHY ARE ASSERTIVENESS/ CONFRONTATION SKILLS IMPORTANT?

Verbal and psychological resistance interrupts the assailant's efforts to intimidate and control his intended victim during the testing stage of an assault. As Dr. Jayne Schuiteman (1989) has written,

Confrontation suggests to the assailant that his intended victim is assertive and confident rather than passive and easily manipulated. A confident, assertive response to testing often deters the assailant because he can't be sure that his intended victim will be easy to overpower and control. If his intended victim doesn't act like an "easy" victim, the assailant often prefers to back down and look for an easier victim. (p. 1)

HOW DO I CONFRONT A POTENTIAL SEXUAL ASSAILANT?

You must demonstrate to the assailant, in a firm and direct manner, that you know what he or she's doing, that it offends you, and that you want it stopped immediately.

Nonverbal Principles of Confrontation

Once again, this strategy contains both verbal and nonverbal principles. The nonverbal principles are essentially the same as those practiced in the de-escalation Drills 1 and 3, except that there is a slight difference in the first principle, in that your demeanor should be confident and *vigilant*, as opposed to *attentive*.

Being *attentive* suggests a solicitousness toward the assailant that would be highly inappropriate in a sexual assault situation. A more effective presentation is to appear alert to what's going on and prepared to meet possible dangers.

Verbal Principles of Confrontation

Your verbal response in the testing stage of a potential sexual assault should be distinctly different from that used in a de-escalation situation, where you're trying to establish rapport and connectedness. Assertiveness/ Confrontation is the firm, verbal refusal on the part of the victim to be controlled, intimidated, or manipulated. Anecdotal literature suggests that many women have found it effective to do the following in a strong, firm voice.

1. Name Offensive or Intrusive Behavior

Name the behavior that you find upsetting or offensive. Doing this tells potential assailants that you're aware of their intentions. Be clear and direct, and don't use qualifiers, such as "I think," "please," "if you don't mind," "sort of," and so on.

Here are some examples: "You are standing too close to me," "I'm uncomfortable with all of the questions you're asking about my personal life," and "You're trying to manipulate/ control/intimidate me."

2. Clearly Communicate Expectations

Tell the assailant exactly how you want him or her to change his or her behavior. Use direct commands so there's no chance of being misunderstood, or of your attacker continuing to negotiate or manipulate you.

Examples might include "Leave me alone," "Take your hands off me," "I'd like you to leave this house."

Put the naming statements together with the commands. For instance, you might say, "You're standing too close to me. Move away!" or "You're using a threatening tone of voice. Don't talk to me in that manner." Schuiteman goes on to say,

By confronting an assailant or harasser you are saying that you will not tolerate inappropriate behavior, that you will not be silent, that you will not be fooled, and that you are not a passive individual. Confrontation works because most assailants would rather back down and find an easier victim than risk an unsuccessful assault. Confrontation is a powerful strategy. Rather than giving power to the assailant, take on power yourself and use confrontation to say "I am a lousy choice for a victim. Don't waste your time on me!" (p. 2)

As with principles of de-escalation, you should see these principles of assertiveness/confrontation as a general guide and not an absolute set of rules. If you sense that any of these suggestions would be counterproductive and dangerous, do *not* implement it. The most reliable guidelines in any situation are your own finely honed intuitions about what might constitute the most appropriate preventive action.

Assertiveness/Confrontation Drills

1. Role-Playing/Bus Stop Scene

Once again, you will need 2 other people to act as (a) a potential sexual assailant and (b) an observer. During the role-playing, the assailant's goal is to establish psychological dominance and control. Your goal as the defender is to attempt to interrupt the assailant's efforts in this regard. Use confrontation skills to bring the following Bus Stop Scene conversation (described earlier under "Immediate Retreat") to an abrupt close. At the conclusion of the role play, the observer gives feedback on the use of nonverbal and verbal principles of assertiveness/confrontation.

Bus Stop Scene Revisited

A female is waiting for a bus late one afternoon in a relatively busy section of town. A man approaches, ostensibly to wait for the same bus, and engages her in conversation. After a number of casual questions, he begins to ask more pointed questions about where and with whom she lives. He also begins to move uncomfortably close to her, even touching her shoulder a couple of times. As his questions become more intrusive and personal, her uneasiness grows.

Success Goal = Minimum of 15 out of 18 possible points

Nonverbal Behaviors (*Gain 1 point each*)

Assume a confident and vigilant demeanor
   Eyes on other person's eyes? _____
   Facial expression neutral? _____
   Posture relaxed and alert? _____
   Movement minimized? _____

Mirror calm
   Breathing deeply and slowly? _____
   Using positive self-talk? _____

Position yourself for safety
 Distance of two arm's lengths? _____
 Body angled at 45 degrees? _____
 Hands free and in front of body? _____
 Using available barriers? _____

Verbal Behaviors (*Gain 4 points each*)

Name the offensive or threatening behavior? _____
Clearly communicate expectations? _____

Your Score = (#) _____ nonverbal points + (#) _____ verbal points = (#) _____ total points

2. Role-Playing/Date Rape

Assertiveness/Confrontation skills are particularly effective and useful in date rape situations. Young women of dating age, including high school and college-age women, are at greatest risk for this form of sexual assault. You may recall that casual and first dates in fact account for nearly half of all rapes on college campuses.

Barry Burkhart and Annette Stanton found that 11 percent of college men had used physical restraint to have intercourse with a woman against her will (1988). Most of these men would not identify themselves as rapists, even though they fulfill the prevailing definition.

According to Mary Koss of Kent State University, assailants in many date rapes are highly sexually aggressive men who use physical force to compel women to have intercourse but who are unlikely to see their act as rape (Koss, 1985). They have oversubscribed to traditional male roles and believe that aggression is normal. They also often subscribe to common myths such as "Women deserve/provoke/enjoy rape" and "Women who say 'no' mean 'yes' " (p. 56).

Victim response to these situations is often characterized by shock, disbelief, confusion, and reluctance to take definitive or even aggressive action with someone they know. However, an absolutely clear, direct, determined, and unambiguous verbal and psychological response may make it more difficult for some date rapists to deceive themselves into believing that this is anything other than violent criminal assault.

Use the same role-play format as described in Drill 1 with one person playing an intended victim of date rape, another playing a potential date rapist, and a third person observing. Act out the following situation.

Date Rape Scene

The defender, a female, is invited by a male friend to play backgammon in his dorm room. On one previous occasion the two have studied together. However, the defender thinks of this person not as a romantic interest, but as a "buddy."

Midway through the game, the potential date rapist, who has been drinking, moves closer to the defender. Abruptly, he begins to touch her face and shoulder in an intimate manner. She tries to draw his attention back to the backgammon game and tells him she's not interested in an intimate relationship with him.

He ignores her and continues to press. She realizes that there's no one else at that end of the hallway and that stereos are blaring at the other end. He grabs her tightly and laughs when she struggles to free herself.

Defender then uses Assertiveness/Confrontation principles to (a) name what is going on and (b) clearly and firmly communicate expectations. For instance, she might say, ''Your continuing to grab at me when I've told you I'm not interested is coercive. Now take your hands off me!'' Make sure your nonverbal behaviors are equally strong and consistent with your verbal message.

If your message is clear and strong enough, the potential date rapist backs off.

Observer then gives feedback on application of the principles and the dynamics of interaction.

Success Goal = Minimum of 15 out of 18 possible points

Nonverbal Behaviors (*Gain 1 point each*)

Assume a confident and vigilant demeanor
Eyes on other person's eyes? _____
Facial expression neutral? _____
Posture relaxed and alert? _____
Movement minimized? _____

Mirror calm
Breathing deeply and slowly? _____
Using positive self-talk? _____

Position yourself for safety
Distance of two arm's lengths? _____
Body angled at 45 degrees? _____
Hands free and in front of body? _____
Using available barriers? _____

Verbal Behaviors (*Gain 4 points each*)

Name the offensive or threatening behavior? _____
Clearly communicate expectations? _____

Your Score = (#) _____ nonverbal points + (#) _____ verbal points = (#) _____ total points

SELF-DEFENSE

Webster defines *self-defense* in very broad terms as the act of defending oneself. Our working definition is somewhat narrower in scope and defines self-defense as the strategy used in response to *physical aggression*. Self-defense, the final option on our Continuum of Response, is a strategy of last resort. Self-defense tactics come into play only when all efforts at avoiding or preventing physical aggression fail.

Why Is Knowledge of Self-Defense Important?

Although your first choice is to avoid or prevent physical aggression whenever you can, this is not always possible. There may be situations in which you can't retreat fast enough, or where your attempts at de-escalation or assertiveness/confrontation are futile. When faced with imminent physical assault, you need to know how to defend yourself in the quickest, most effective manner possible.

How Do I Defend Myself Against Physical Assault?

The general rule of thumb in defending against a physical assault is to do whatever is necessary to break free of the attacker and get to safety. Ideally, your defense will be immediate and effective, minimizing the length of time that you are struggling or grappling with an assailant. It should also reflect the *ethic of least harm*—a commitment to using the least damaging or punishing techniques necessary to deter an attacker while still doing whatever is required to ensure your own safety.

Some believe that the ethic of least harm unfairly holds defenders to a higher ethical standard than attackers and that attackers ''deserve whatever they get.'' These people also often believe that it's okay to deal the aggressor a few extra punishing blows to teach him or her a lesson. However, those few extra blows keep the defender within range of the attacker and consequently at risk longer than necessary. They may also anger and incite an attacker to even greater violence.

From a practical standpoint, to say nothing of the legal and ethical considerations, it simply makes sense to do only the very least necessary —and this includes selecting the least lethal response—to neutralize an attack and get away as quickly as possible. However, once you make a decision about what techniques *are* necessary to deter the attacker, respond unequivocally and without hesitation. Defend yourself with whatever you feel is reasonable and necessary under the circumstances, and do so with conviction, spirit, and an absolute determination to stop the assault.

Step 4 Evasive Sidestep

As you begin your study of self-defense, you'll need to learn its terminology. Even familiar terms may have slightly different meanings in this context, so pay close attention as the language of self-defense is introduced throughout this step.

Your study begins with an *evasive sidestep*, one of a number of *neutralizing* techniques designed to render an attack ineffective. They include such tactics as evasions, blocks (see Step 5), and hold breaks (see Steps 9-13).

Evasions are maneuvers that involve removing your body from the line of attack and avoiding physical contact entirely. Running, jumping, dodging, slipping, ducking, and sidestepping are all evasions.

Evasions are frequently used when an attack is initiated from outside of striking range—the attacker can't reach you without taking one or more closing steps. The ground to be covered between you and the attacker, called the *critical distance zone* (CDZ), often provides you time to see the attack coming and move out of the way. This critical distance zone needs to be at least two arm's lengths, in order

to buy you enough time to react before you are seized or struck (see Figure 4.1). The most common evasion is simply running toward safety (when that avenue of escape is not blocked by the assailant).

WHY IS AN EVASIVE SIDESTEP IMPORTANT?

In some situations, the attacker stands between the defender and the avenue of escape. The evasive sidestep lets the defender get around the attacker and closer to an exit.

HOW TO DO AN EVASIVE SIDESTEP

The preparation phase of this technique is called the *defensive stance* (see Figure 4.2). You will assume this stance in preparation for not only evasive sidestep, but for most of the defensive and offensive techniques presented later. You always assume the stance the instant that the attacker initiates physical aggression. Just before this, you may very well be in the defensive posture shown previously in Figure 3.1. The defensive posture is easily

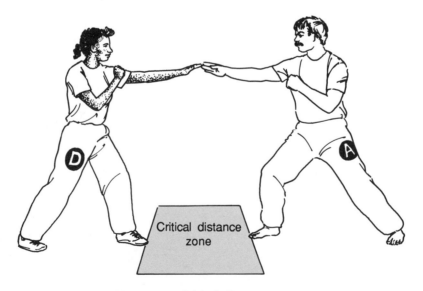

Figure 4.1 Critical distance zone.

Figure 4.2   Defensive stance.

and quickly transformed to the defensive stance by simply widening the base of support and bringing your hands up in front of your body for more complete protection of vulnerable areas.

Assume the defensive stance by placing feet one and one-half shoulder-widths apart. Now draw one foot straight back and angle your body at 45 degrees. Point your lead foot straight ahead as you angle your back foot slightly outward. Distribute your weight evenly over both feet. Bend your knees slightly, straighten your spine, and turn your face to look squarely at the attacker.

The position of your arms in a defensive stance is called your *guard*. Bend your arms at 90 to 120 degrees, and tuck your elbows close to your body. Your forward arm (called the *lead arm*) is a little higher and further from the body than the back arm (called the *trailing arm*). Your lead fist is placed no higher than your throat in order not to obstruct your vision. Loosely fist your hands, and make sure that the little finger edge of your fist is facing outward. Maintain this guard to provide maximum coverage of vulnerable areas along your *centerline*.

''Centerline'' refers to the 8- to 12-inch–wide zone running down the front of your body from the crown to the pubis. Some of the most vulnerable areas of the body, such as the head and face, throat, solar plexus,

bladder, and groin are clustered along this zone (see Figure 4.3a). The positioning of the guard, as well as the angling of the body in a defensive stance, helps protect these vital areas (see Figure 4.3b).

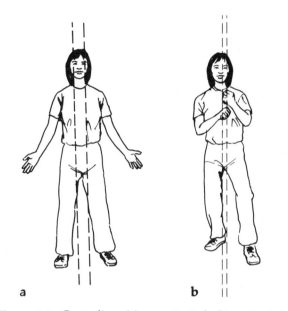

Figure 4.3   Centerline: (a) unprotected, (b) protected.

In your defensive stance (see Figure 4.4), you may present your right or your left side forward, whichever feels most comfortable. Many right-handed people prefer to lead with their left so that their strongest arm is trailing. (Note: Trailing-arm techniques are usually stronger because they incorporate greater hip rotation. Trailing with the dominant arm increases the power still more.)

To do the sidestep, first imagine an invisible line connecting you to the attacker. This is called the *connecting line*. Watch as the attacker moves down that line toward you. When she or he has nearly reached you, abruptly step to the side.

Another approach is to imagine that you are standing in the center of a giant clock face. The attack is launched from the 12 position. As the attacker approaches the center, you can move to either the 9 or to the 3 position. Your second step is toward the 12, if that is where your avenue of escape is.

Whether you step to 9 or 3 will depend on the precise location of your avenue of escape. Obviously, you'll want to step in the direction that brings you nearer to it. As long as the attack trajectory is straight in or descending, a step in either direction is effective.

Premature movement will allow the attacker to track you. Hold your ground until the very last moment in order to ensure that the attacker's momentum will carry him or her past you.

The step to the side should be a lunging step—one capable of carrying you nearly out of the attacker's range. If you are stepping to the left, reach with the left leg and push off with the right leg, and vice versa. Immediately step straight ahead with your other foot to carry you toward your avenue of escape.

As you do the sidestep, keep your spine erect and your guard up. After you've evaded your attacker, immediately retreat to safety. *Look* in the direction in which you're running.

Figure 4.4 Keys to Success: *Evasive Sidestep*

**Preparation Phase
(Defensive Stance)**

1. Body angled at 45 degrees ____
2. Feet 1-1/2 shoulder-widths apart ____
3. Lead foot pointing straight ahead ____
4. Back foot angled slightly outward ____
5. Weight evenly distributed over both feet ____
6. Knees slightly bent ____
7. Spine erect ____
8. Elbows bent 90 degrees and held in front of chest ____
9. Lead hand high and outside ____
10. Trailing hand lower and inside ____
11. Elbows tucked in ____
12. Hands loosely fisted ____
13. Wrist line straight ____
14. Little finger edge of fist toward attacker ____
15. Face turned toward attacker ____

a

Execution Phase

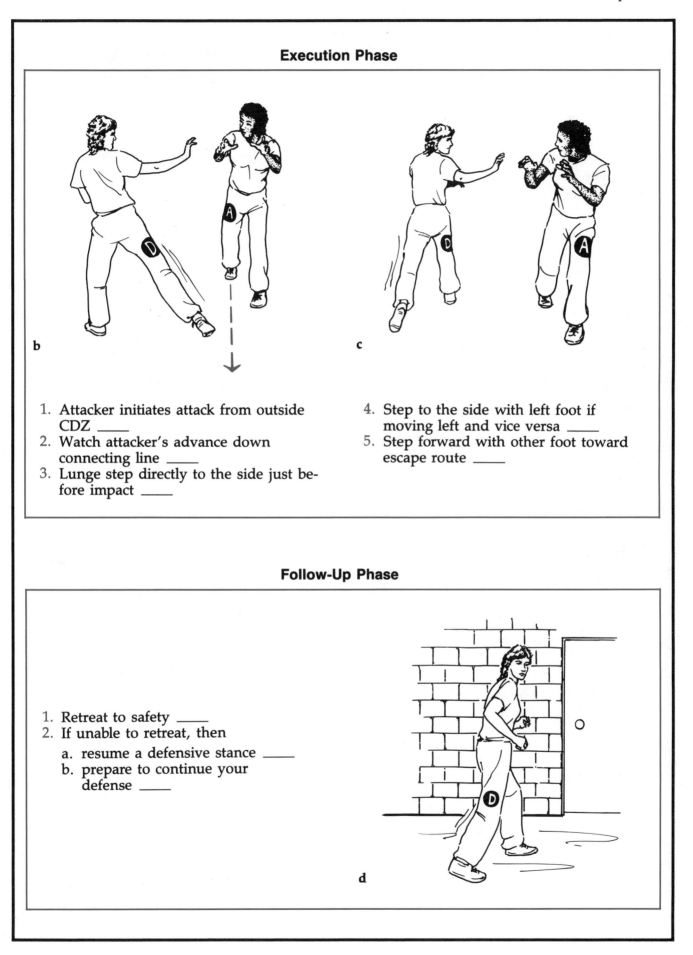

b

c

1. Attacker initiates attack from outside CDZ ____
2. Watch attacker's advance down connecting line ____
3. Lunge step directly to the side just before impact ____

4. Step to the side with left foot if moving left and vice versa ____
5. Step forward with other foot toward escape route ____

Follow-Up Phase

1. Retreat to safety ____
2. If unable to retreat, then
   a. resume a defensive stance ____
   b. prepare to continue your defense ____

d

Detecting Errors in an Evasive Sidestep

Sidestep errors are most often related to difficulties in monitoring the attacker's advance and timing your defense. Remember that it's important not to step too soon or too late.

While quickness depends in large part on the explosive power in your legs, attention to biomechanical details such as posture will help significantly.

ERROR 🚫

CORRECTION

1. You're bending at the waist as you sidestep.

1. Keep your spine erect as you step. Piking or bending on your first step will slow your second one.

2. You're spinning around between your first and second steps.

3. You're dropping your guard as you sidestep.

4. Your attacker is able to track you as you step to the side.

5. Your attacker is running over you.

2. This is caused by turning your head and looking in the direction in which you're stepping. Keep your eyes on your attacker.

3. This could be dangerous. The combination of evasive footwork and shielding the centerline is most effective in keeping you safe. Keep your guard between you and your attacker as you move.

4. You're moving too soon. Wait until the attacker is just short of striking range before stepping off the connecting line.

5. You're either not moving early enough or you're moving too slowly. Wait until the last second, then bound off the line. Make your movement sudden and explosive.

Evasive Sidestep Drills

1. Solo Sidestep Drill

Assume a defensive stance at least 10 feet in front of a large, full-length mirror and practice doing evasive sidesteps. Monitor your posture and maintain an effective guard. Practice stepping to the 9 and the 12 clock face positions, then to 3 and 12. Work on making your movements sudden and explosive.

   Note: It doesn't matter which leg is forward in determining whether to step to the left or right. In an assault situation, you would step right or left, depending on which brought you nearer to your avenue of escape.

Success Goals =

   a. 25 correct evasive sidesteps to your left (9 o'clock)

   b. 25 correct evasive sidesteps to your right (3 o'clock)

Your Score =

   a. (#)_____ correct evasive sidesteps to the left

   b. (#)_____ correct evasive sidesteps to the right

2. Triangle Drill

This drill is done with a partner and develops a sense of range and timing with respect to sidesteps. Face your partner from a distance of two arm's lengths (i.e., just outside the critical distance zone). One of you is designated an "attacker," and the other the "defender." With a nod of the head, the defender signals his or her readiness, and the attacker charges down the connecting line with arms outstretched. At the last second, the defender executes an evasive sidestep. After completing the step to 12, the defender instantly turns to face the attacker again. The defender now stands where the attacker originally stood, and the attacker stands in the defender's original position. (The step to 12 can be slightly angled toward the attacker for the purposes of this drill.) The positions have changed, but not the roles. The same defender signals his or her readiness, and the attacker charges again. An evasive sidestep brings the defender back to

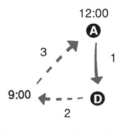

a. Sidestep to defender's left

or

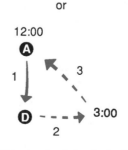

b. Sidestep to defender's right

where he or she started. The defender continues to signal and respond with evasive sidesteps for 25 repetitions. After 25 successful executions of this technique, the roles should be reversed.

Success Goal = 25 successful evasive sidesteps in each direction (left and right)

Your Score =

(#)_____ successful evasive sidesteps to the left

(#)_____ successful evasive side-steps to the right

3. Triangle Drill With Shout

A variation of the previous Triangle Drill involves the attacker shouting as she or he charges down the connecting line. The added shout frequently startles and momentarily disorients the defender. It also adds to the realism of the attack. Incorporating the shout into the Triangle Drill helps defenders work on overcoming their confusion or startledness by noise and moving quickly into action.

We call this capacity to quickly overcome panic and focus on the details of our defense *recall under stress*. This capacity is honed and strengthened by beginning the drill with a noisy attack and adding progressively more startling stressors to your practice. Remember that the defender still initiates the charge and shout by a nod of the head.

Success Goal = 25 successful evasive sidesteps in response to noisy, planned attacks

Your Score = (#)_____ successful evasive sidesteps in response to noisy, planned attacks

4. Triangle Drill With Spontaneous Attacks

This is yet another variation on the Triangle Drill. It works the same way as the version just described, except that this time the attacker, not the defender, decides when to charge. Once positions are taken on the connecting line (i.e., immediately following the completion of an evasive sidestep), the attacker can charge at any time. In this way, the defender learns to respond to sudden and aggressive movement from the attacker. The fact that the defender does not control precisely when the charge comes increases stress and helps develop the capacity for quick thinking and timely reaction, or recall under stress.

Success Goal = 25 successful evasive sidesteps in response to noisy, spontaneous attacks

Your Score = (#)_____ successful evasive sidesteps in response to noisy, spontaneous attacks

5. *Milling Drill*

In this drill, four or more participants mill around randomly and maintain a minimum distance of two arm's lengths from each other. Anyone can be an attacker or a defender. To attack, you point at another and shout, "You!" Both of you make eye contact and freeze. You then suddenly rush forward with a shout. The defender executes an evasive sidestep. Once the defender has evaded the attack, you both begin to mill again until one or the other is moved to attack or called to defend. The drill increases stress still more because of the number of potential attackers and a constantly shifting connecting line.

Success Goal = 2 minutes of effective sidesteps in response to charging attacks while milling

Your Score = (#)_____ minutes of milling using effective sidesteps

Evasive Sidestep
Keys to Success Checklist

Have a teacher or trained observer use the checklist in Figure 4.4 to evaluate key elements of this first neutralizing technique. Ask them to carefully check the details of your defensive stance, which is critical for all future techniques.

Step 5 **Blocks**

Now that you've learned how to evade attacks whenever possible, you're ready to learn how to block. A *block* is an arm maneuver designed to deflect an incoming attack from its target. Whereas evasions were used in response to attacks initiated from outside the critical distance zone (CDZ), blocks are more often used in response to punches and other strikes originating from within the CDZ. You can deflect strikes in any direction—high, low, or to the sides—although the most efficient and easily learned blocks are to either side of your body. In this step you'll learn how and when to use two basic blocks—the *outside block* and the *inside block*.

WHY ARE BLOCKS IMPORTANT?

Blocks are neutralizing techniques that enable you to deflect an incoming strike away from the vulnerable organs and structures clustered along your centerline. These quick and effective redirects are especially important for protecting your face, throat, and solar plexus.

Knowing both an outside and an inside block enables you to deflect an attack to either side of your body. Which of these blocks you use in an assault situation will depend upon a number of factors. Among these are the angle of attack, the position of your guard, and your intended follow-up to the block. Choosing between these two blocks is a strategic decision that you'll learn to make a little later, once you've learned how to block.

HOW TO EXECUTE AN OUTSIDE BLOCK

Begin by assuming the defensive stance you learned previously in Step 3.

To do an *outside block*, sweep your forearm to the side of your body and away from your centerline. This is powered by slight trunk rotation in the same direction as the arm sweep. Keep your elbow bent at a right angle and your forearm nearly perpendicular to the ground. Just before impact with an incoming punch, rotate your forearm outward to a palm-out position. The ulnar edge of your forearm, just above the wrist bone, is the striking surface. The target of your block is the attacker's wrist or forearm, and you should make impact when the punch is about two thirds of the way to its target. On impact, tighten your fist and continue the movement of your forearm to the side. You must generate enough force to knock the incoming punch off its trajectory and away from your centerline. On the other hand, go no further than necessary to ensure that you're not hit.

Once the block is complete, return to a guard position in order to minimize the length of time your centerline is unprotected. Retreat immediately or prepare to continue your defense. The outside block is most effective when used to deflect an incoming strike thrown with the attacker's arm directly opposite your blocking arm. This is called *mirror-image* or *same-side blocking*. So you should use a left outside block to deflect a right-hand punch, whereas you should use a right outside block to deflect a left-hand punch.

An outside block can be raised or lowered to deflect punches thrown to the head and throat region, called *high outside block,* or to the midsection, called *middle outside block.* Your forearm should be nearly vertical in either case, and the point of contact is still wrist-to-wrist.

In addition to proper biomechanics, effective blocking requires good observational skills. The earlier you're able to determine what kind of punch is being thrown to which target and with which hand, the greater the chances that you'll deflect the strike. Train your eyes on the attacker's eyes, but maintain an awareness of his or her entire body. Keep your vision soft and receptive. Soft vision is passive and avoids a hard, narrow focus on any one part of the body. Because it is inclusive of the entire body it enables you to note an attack in its earliest stages. You'll notice movement in the attacker's hips and shoulders before you see the action in the hands. Hips and shoulders are referred to as *general monitoring points,* while hands are *specific monitoring points.* The general points will telegraph the attacker's intentions earlier, and close attention to them will increase your chances of responding with timely and appropriate blocks.

HOW TO EXECUTE AN INSIDE BLOCK

Whereas an outside block involves movement of the blocking arm away from your centerline, an *inside block* crosses your centerline to deflect the attack to the opposite side.

Begin by assuming a defensive stance. To block, sweep your bent arm across your centerline and toward your opposite shoulder. Just before intercepting the incoming attack, rotate your arm to a palm-in position. This ensures that the striking surface is the ulnar edge of your forearm, just above the wrist bone. Continue the movement just far enough to deflect the attack to the side. As you block with one arm, protect your centerline with the other. Return to a guard position as soon as you complete the block.

Note that this technique is launched by rotating your trunk in the same direction in which you're blocking. In addition to ensuring a more powerful block, trunk rotation takes you out of the line of attack and renders your centerline less accessible.

As with outside blocks, inside blocks are usually mirror-image techniques (see Figure 5.1). They also require good observational skills. Soft vision and an awareness of shoulder and hip movement will give you advance warning of the timing and direction of the attack and will allow you to prepare to respond effectively.

Figure 5.1 Keys to Success: *Blocks*

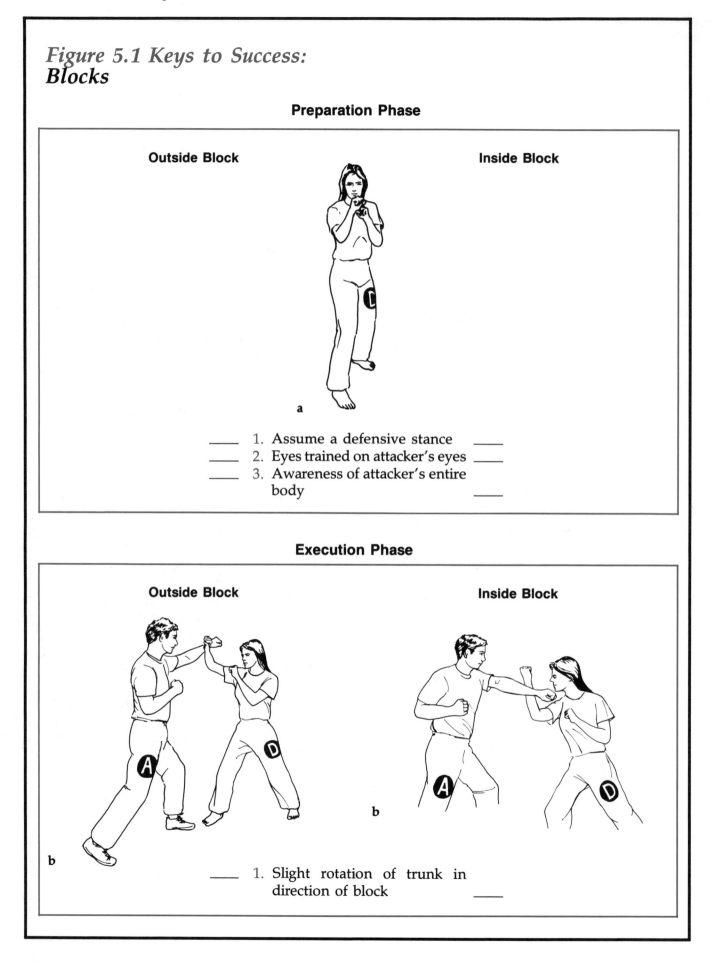

Preparation Phase

Outside Block   **Inside Block**

a

____ 1. Assume a defensive stance ____
____ 2. Eyes trained on attacker's eyes ____
____ 3. Awareness of attacker's entire body

                                        ____

Execution Phase

Outside Block   **Inside Block**

b   b

____ 1. Slight rotation of trunk in direction of block

                                        ____

Outside Block	**Inside Block**

2. Sweep vertical forearm to the side ＿＿＿

2. Sweep forearm across centerline, toward opposite shoulder ＿＿＿

＿＿＿ 3. Use arm opposite attacking limb (mirror-image) ＿＿＿

＿＿＿ 4. Elbow bent 90 degrees ＿＿＿

＿＿＿ 5. Forearm nearly perpendicular to the floor ＿＿＿

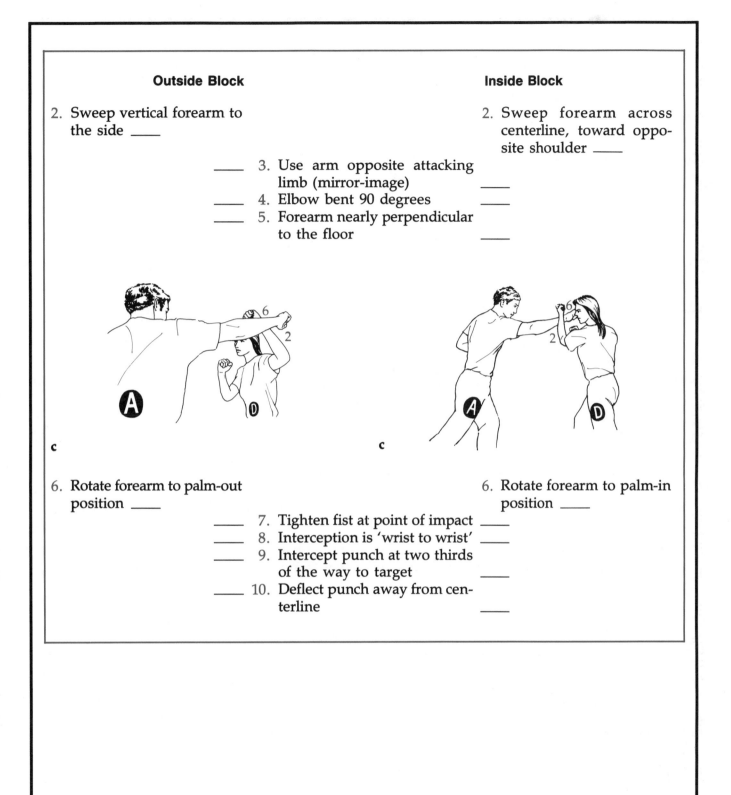

c   c

6. Rotate forearm to palm-out position ＿＿＿

6. Rotate forearm to palm-in position ＿＿＿

＿＿＿ 7. Tighten fist at point of impact ＿＿＿

＿＿＿ 8. Interception is 'wrist to wrist' ＿＿＿

＿＿＿ 9. Intercept punch at two thirds of the way to target ＿＿＿

＿＿＿ 10. Deflect punch away from centerline ＿＿＿

Follow-Up Phase

Outside Block   Inside Block

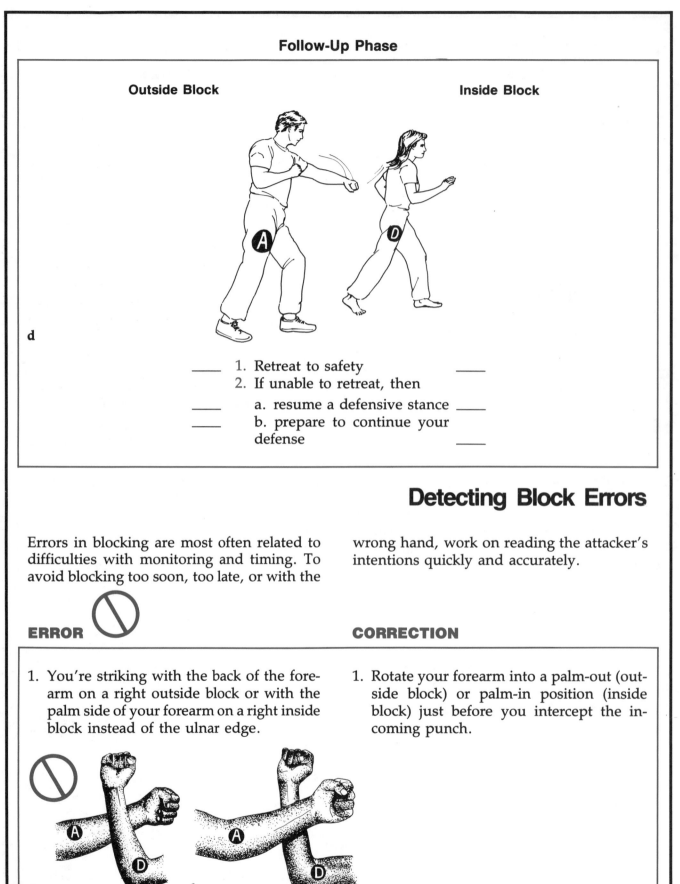

d

_____   1. Retreat to safety   _____
        2. If unable to retreat, then

_____   a. resume a defensive stance _____
_____   b. prepare to continue your
              defense   _____

Detecting Block Errors

Errors in blocking are most often related to difficulties with monitoring and timing. To avoid blocking too soon, too late, or with the wrong hand, work on reading the attacker's intentions quickly and accurately.

ERROR   **CORRECTION**

1. You're striking with the back of the forearm on a right outside block or with the palm side of your forearm on a right inside block instead of the ulnar edge.

1. Rotate your forearm into a palm-out (outside block) or palm-in position (inside block) just before you intercept the incoming punch.

a   b

ERROR 🚫   **CORRECTION**

2. Even though you're blocking in a timely manner, you're still getting hit.

2. You are not generating enough force to deflect the punch from its path. Increase trunk rotation to increase power of the sweep and take your centerline off the punch trajectory. Sustain sweep beyond point of impact to make sure the punch clears your centerline.

3. You're blocking too late, as evidenced by the fact that the attacker's arm is fully extended before you block. (In a real situation, you'd be hit!)

3. Don't drop your guard. Keep it in front of your chest and ready for use the instant an attack is thrown. Maintain soft vision and awareness of attacker's entire body. This should help you read cues earlier and block in a timely manner.

4. You're doing cross-body rather than mirror-image blocking.

4. Determine sooner which hand will be used to punch by monitoring shoulder movement more effectively. Remember that right and left punches are indicated by forward movement of right and left shoulders, respectively.

Blocking Drills

1. Solo Blocking Drill

The purpose of this drill is to begin to develop a feel for these blocks, without the additional challenges of timing and range that are introduced with partner work.

   Assume a defensive stance, preferably in front of a full-length mirror. Quickly attend to details of the defensive stance. Then throw half-speed outside blocks, alternating right and left. Take note of all of the details of the execution phase. Finish each block with a rapid return to the guard position.

Then try the outside blocks with your eyes closed in order to develop an even better feel for the technique.

Now repeat this procedure, using the proper technique for inside blocks, first with your eyes open and then with eyes closed.

Success Goals =

a. 40 total outside blocks

    20 with eyes open and proper technique (10 to each side)

    20 with eyes closed and proper technique (10 to each side)

b. 40 total inside blocks

    20 with eyes open and proper technique (10 to each side)

    20 with eyes closed and proper technique (10 to each side)

Your Score =

a. (#)_____ outside blocks with eyes open and proper technique

   (#)_____ outside blocks with eyes closed and proper technique

b. (#)_____ inside blocks with eyes open and proper technique

   (#)_____ inside blocks with eyes closed and proper technique

2. Predictable Punch Drill

You and your partner will stand facing each other in defensive stances. It doesn't matter which side you choose to be the lead, although many people prefer to put the left leg and arm forward.

One person plays the attacker and will throw slow-speed punches toward the defender's nose. These punches should move in a straight line from the guard position to a spot 2 inches in front of the target. Stopping short of the actual target at this point is to prevent your striking and possibly injuring the defender whose block is unsuccessful. The attacker alternates right and left punches, so as to make them more predictable. The defender can then concentrate on intercepting each incoming punch with correctly executed and well-timed blocks. Once each incoming punch is deflected, the defender quickly retracts the blocking arm into guard position.

Do the Predictable Punch Drill using outside blocks until you have reached your Success Goal. Then repeat the drill using inside blocks.

Note: Wearing forearm pads will reduce soreness resulting from lengthy impact drills. If these are unavailable, block lightly to spare your partner's forearms.

Success Goals =

a. 42 out of 50 total punches blocked successfully and correctly with outside block

    21 out of 25 right outside blocks

    21 out of 25 left outside blocks

   b. 42 out of 50 total punches blocked successfully and correctly with inside block

       21 out of 25 right inside blocks

       21 out of 25 left inside blocks

Your Score =

   a. (#)_____ right outside blocks

      (#)_____ left outside blocks

   b. (#)_____ right inside blocks

      (#)_____ left inside blocks

3. Monitoring Drill

In this drill, you'll focus on observational skills. You and your partner stand facing each other in defensive stances. As soon as the defender reads the attacker's intention to punch, he or she shouts ''Now!'' Attacker confirms that she or he was about to punch by saying ''Yes.'' Defender should shout before the punch has traveled halfway to the target.

Possible cues for reading the attacker's intentions include shoulder, hip, and hand movement. Even earlier cues might be changes in expression, shift of the guard, or increased tension in the body. Some of these are much more subtle than others. Monitoring intention is easier when the defender maintains a soft, receptive vision and an awareness of the attacker's entire body. Note: The defender makes no effort to block in these drills. As soon as the defender shouts, the attacker aborts the punch.

A variation on this drill requiring even greater perceptiveness is to identify which side the punch is coming from by shouting ''Left'' or ''Right'' instead of ''Now.''

Success Goals =

   a. 20 out of 25 successful monitorings of attacker's intention to throw a punch as evidenced by defender shouting ''Now'' before the punch has traveled halfway to target

   b. 20 out of 25 successful monitorings of attacker's intention to throw a left or right punch as evidenced by defender's shouting ''Left'' or ''Right'' before the punch has traveled halfway to target

Your Score =

   a. (#)_____ successful monitorings of intention to punch

   b. (#)_____ successful monitorings of whether punch will be thrown with right or left hand

4. Unpredictable Punch Drill

Stand facing your partner in a defensive stance. Just as in the Predictable Punch Drill, your partner will throw slow-speed straight-line punches at a regular rhythm. Instead of alternating punches, however, he or she will throw them in no particular order. You'll need to determine the hand being used to punch, then block using the same-side, or mirror-image arm. As your skill in anticipating and deflecting punches increases, your partner should gradually increase the speed of the punches up to 3/4 of maximum speed. Whatever the speed of the punches, they should be thrown with a regular, predictable rhythm. Use outside blocks only until you've reached the Success Goal, then switch to inside blocks.

Success Goals =

 a. 40 out of 50 punches blocked correctly with a mirror image outside block

 b. 40 out of 50 punches blocked correctly with mirror image inside block

Your Score =

 a. (#)_____ out of 50 punches blocked with correctly executed outside block

 b. (#)_____ out of 50 punches blocked with correctly executed inside block

5. Broken Rhythm Drill

This drill is the same as the Unpredictable Punch Drill, except that the attacker throws punches in an irregular rhythm to make them even less predictable. Attacker should throw punches at slow speed until you're blocking consistently and correctly. Attacker gradually increases speed to 3/4 of maximum speed. Use outside blocks until you've reached the Success Goal, then switch to inside blocks.

Success Goals =

 a. 40 out of 50 punches deflected with outside blocks

 b. 40 out of 50 punches deflected with inside blocks

Your Score =

 a. (#)_____ out of 50 punches deflected with outside blocks

 b. (#)_____ out of 50 punches deflected with inside blocks

6. Variable Block Drill

Knowing both the inside block and the outside block enables you to deflect an incoming strike in either direction. As stated earlier, your choice regarding whether to block away from or across your centerline is influenced by your intended follow-up to the block, the angle of attack, and the positioning of your guard.

 For instance, the situation may be one in which you decide that a simple block followed by a hasty retreat will probably not be enough to stop the assault. You may feel it necessary to follow up your block with counterattacks (strikes of your own) to stun the attacker enough to allow time for you to retreat safely. In this case, you'll probably decide to use an outside block. Notice that upon completion of this block, your attacker's centerline is exposed and your non-blocking hand is available for strikes. For this reason this block is said to establish the *angle of opportunity*. Bear in mind that the attacker is also in position to avail him- or herself of these opportunities.

In contrast, the inside block is associated with the *angle of safety*. At the point of interception and beyond, the attacker's punching arm and your blocking arm shield your respective center-lines. In addition, both your nonblocking hands are poorly positioned for centerline strikes. The advantage of an inside block is that it leaves you (and your attacker) in a more protected position. It also sets up a quick and somewhat safer retreat.

In sum, the outside block is frequently used in combination with counterattacks because it provides immediate and direct access to the attacker's centerline. It is somewhat risky in that the attacker also has immediate access to *your* centerline. The more protective inside block allows for a quick retreat immediately following the block.

In previous drills, you've focused on one block at a time. In this drill you'll choose either the outside or the inside block to deflect the punch from its trajectory.

The attacker throws slow- to medium-speed punches with whichever hand he or she chooses. You respond with an outside or an inside block. Note how slight changes in the angle of attack, as well as the precise placement of your own guard in relation to the incoming punch, help determine which block you'll use. Freeze in the completed block position for a second and identify the angle—whether that of safety (inside block) or opportunity (outside block). Remember that both inside and outside blocks are mirror-image blocks.

The attacker should punch slowly at first and pause briefly between each punch. As your blocking becomes more proficient, the attacker should increase speed but continue punching in a controlled fashion at all times.

Success Goal = 3 minutes continuous blocking using variable technique

Your Score = (#)_____ minutes continuous blocking using variable technique

7. Circle Retreat Drill

An attacker seldom throws punches from a stationary position in an assault situation. It is more likely that your attacker will be advancing toward you rapidly while throwing multiple punches.

A common defense is to simply move straight back. If your avenue of escape is directly behind you, this is an appropriate and useful move. If the attacker is blocking the exit, however, you're better off retreating in a circular fashion. A circling retreat makes it more difficult for the attacker to land a punch. It also enables you to eventually maneuver into position to break and run.

This drill offers an opportunity to circle retreat and block at the same time. Before you begin the drill, make sure you have ample room for circling. Designate a corner of the room as the avenue of escape. To start, the

attacker takes a position between you, the defender, and your avenue of escape.

On cue, the attacker advances steadily toward you, throwing slow- to medium-speed punches. Circle to either side, changing directions as often as you need to to stay out of range of the punches. Keep your guard up at all times to shield your centerline. As punches come within striking range, block them with either outside or inside blocks. If the punch is thrown from too great a distance to be a threat, don't rush in to block it. Simply maintain your shield and keep dancing out of range.

Continue circling until you're nearer your avenue of escape than your attacker is. Break and run at the first opportunity.

Remember, the circling retreat is used to stay out of range. Your blocks in this case are your backup, or secondary defense. Use them when the attacker has closed in enough to be able to strike you.

A variation of this drill is to have the attackers shout as they advance and punch. Because this increases the stress on defenders, it offers an opportunity to practice defense in a more realistic fashion. Add the shout only after you've practiced the skill without it.

Success Goals =

    a. 3 sets of 15 seconds of a circling retreat with blocks as needed and a dash to safety

    b. 1 set of 15 seconds of the same, with attacker shouting

Your Score =

    a. _____ 3 sets of 15 seconds without shouting, completed (yes? or no?)

    b. _____ 1 set of 15 seconds with shouting, completed (yes? or no?)

Blocks
Keys to Success Checklist

Have your teacher or a trained observer evaluate both observational and biomechanical elements of your inside and outside blocks using the checklist within Figure 5.1. Good observational skills will be evidenced by timely, mirror-image blocks. Key biomechanical elements to look for include trunk rotation, vertical forearm positioning, last-minute wrist rotation, wrist-to-wrist interception, effective deflection of attack away from vulnerable targets, and quick return to a guard position.

Step 6 Front-Facing Counterattacks

In general, *counterattack* refers to the act of responding to an incoming attack with an attack of your own. In this book, counterattacks refer specifically to strikes used by the defender to discourage further aggressive action by the attacker. Your training in counterattacks begins with five front-facing techniques—punch, eye gouge, palm-heel strikes, web strike, and front snap kick.

These strikes concentrate a great deal of ballistic force to small and vulnerable body targets. Depending on the target and the degree of force generated, a counterattack may result in moderate discomfort, serious and riveting pain, minor or major injury, or possibly even death to the person receiving the blow. Given their potential for inflicting serious injury, the defender will usually attempt all other applicable responses before opting to use these techniques. Indeed, the law requires that you use only the degree of force that is reasonable and necessary to defend yourself.

WHY ARE COUNTERATTACKS IMPORTANT?

In many assault situations, a neutralizing technique such as an evasion, block, or simple release is simply not enough to deter an attacker. Fast, accurate, and powerful strikes thrown to parts of the body that are particularly vulnerable to pain and injury are usually effective in discouraging the assailant from pressing the assault and will give you time to escape.

Because you can be attacked from any direction, you need to be able to strike an assailant standing in front, behind, or beside you.

Although an attack can come from any direction, many of them occur when you're face-to-face with an aggressor. Even when attacked initially from the side or from behind, you may end up looking the attacker squarely in the eye. In Steps 7 and 8, you'll be learning counterattacks useful in dealing with attacks coming from directly behind and beside you.

BODY TARGETS AND BODY WEAPONS

Effective counterattacking requires a knowledge of *body targets* and *body weapons*, in other words, knowing what parts of your body can be used to strike available targets on the assailant.

Body Targets

A blow to any part of the body may cause injury or pain, but certain areas are particularly vulnerable. We call these areas *body targets* (see Figures 6.1a and b).

Targets of the head and neck region include the eyes, nose, chin, throat, side of the neck, base of the skull, ears, jaw, and temples. Because of the extreme susceptibility of this

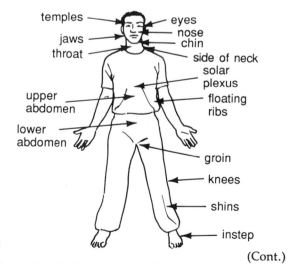

(Cont.)

Figure 6.1 Body targets: (a) front view, (b) rear view.

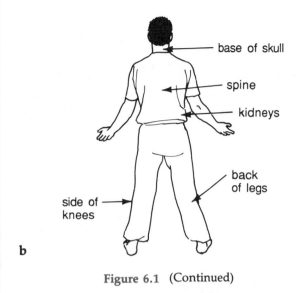

b

Figure 6.1   (Continued)

region to serious injury, a strike to the head or neck may constitute deadly force. Trunk targets are fewer and somewhat less vulnerable. They include the solar plexus, floating ribs, kidneys, spine, upper abdomen, lower abdomen, and groin. Peripheral targets, although fairly susceptible to disabling techniques, require much more precise and accurate targeting. These targets are the knees (all sides), shins, and insteps.

Body Weapons

It's helpful to think of having six *body weapons* or parts of your own body that can be used to throw counterattacks to selected body targets (see Figure 6.2). These body weapons

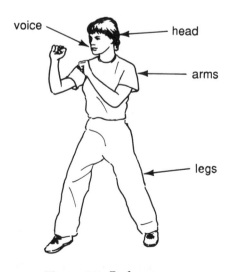

Figure 6.2   Body weapons.

consist of two upper limbs for striking, two lower limbs for leg techniques, your head for butting and biting, and your voice.

HOW TO PUNCH

A punch is the most versatile of all strikes and can be directed to any of several body targets. It can be thrown in a straight line (called a *straight-line punch*) or in a curved line (called a *hook*).

A punch can be thrown with either hand. When thrown with the lead hand, the punch is referred to as a *lead punch* or a *jab*. When thrown with the trailing hand, it is called a *reverse punch*. Of these two, the latter is more powerful because of the greater trunk rotation involved (see Figure 6.3). In this book you'll concentrate on learning lead and reverse straight-line punches thrown to the nose, chin, throat, or solar plexus.

Begin by assuming a defensive stance. Hands should be loosely fisted in this preparation phase. Keep your fingers curled, with your thumb outside and perpendicular to the fingers. Your wrist line should be straight.

Lead Punch

Launch your *lead punch* with a sharp, short rotation of the trunk in the direction of the target. Keep in mind that the target will be the nose, chin, throat, or, less often, the solar plexus. Keep your hand loosely fisted and move it in a straight line. On impact with the target, tighten the fist and rotate it into a palm-down position. Make sure your arm is bent and your wrist line is straight. Note that the striking surface is the top portion of the first two knuckles, assuming you contact the target with a very compact and firm fist. To maximize the effectiveness of the punch, think of punching *through* the target to a point 6 inches beyond it.

Reverse Punch

The more powerful reverse punch is launched with somewhat greater trunk rotation. Movement flows from the large muscle groups of the trunk and shoulders through progressively smaller muscle groups in the arms, wrist, and hand. This movement from the inside out results in the generation of considerable force at the point of impact. Targets are the same as for lead punches, although the more powerful reverse punch has greater impact to the solar plexus than a lead punch.

If you are able to retreat after a single punch, do so. However, retreat may not always be possible. In this case, keep your guard up and prepare to throw additional blocks and counterattacks until you're able to retreat.

Figure 6.3 Keys to Success: Punch

Preparation Phase

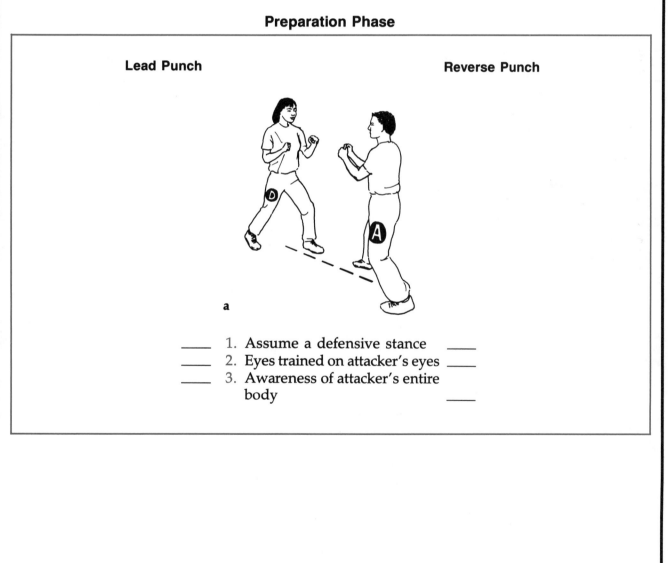

Lead Punch

Reverse Punch

a

____ 1. Assume a defensive stance ____
____ 2. Eyes trained on attacker's eyes ____
____ 3. Awareness of attacker's entire
      body   ____

Execution Phase

Lead Punch   **Reverse Punch**

b

b

c

c

_____ 1. Rotate trunk to launch technique (greater on reverse punch)   _____

_____ 2. Extend lead (trailing) hand toward target (nose, chin, throat, or solar plexus)   _____

_____ 3. Maintain straight-line trajectory   _____

_____ 4. Keep elbows in and behind fist (don't wing)   _____

_____ 5. At impact, tighten fist   _____

_____ 6. Rotate fist into palm-down position   _____

_____ 7. Keep elbow slightly bent   _____

_____ 8. Maintain a straight wrist line _____

_____ 9. Striking surface is top two knuckles   _____

_____ 10. Punch through the target   _____

Follow-Up Phase

Lead Punch		Reverse Punch
____	1. Retreat to safety	____
	2. If unable to retreat, then	
____	a. return to defensive stance (guard repositioned)	____
____	b. prepare to continue defense	____

Detecting Errors in a Punch

Inadequate attention to biomechanical details frequently results in injury to the hand and wrist. Here are a number of very common errors committed by beginners.

ERROR / **CORRECTION**

ERROR	CORRECTION
1. Your punch has little power or effect.	1. Try for the fullest possible hip rotation. Accelerate your punch as you move from the inside out—from rotation of hips to shoulders to arms to wrist and hand. Make sure you're close enough to target so that your elbow is still bent at impact. Then continue extending arm in an effort to punch through the target.
2. You're hooking your punches, rather than maintaining a straight-line trajectory.	2. Keep your elbows in and traveling behind your punch. Premature rotation into a palm-down position will cause you to wing your elbows and hook your punch.

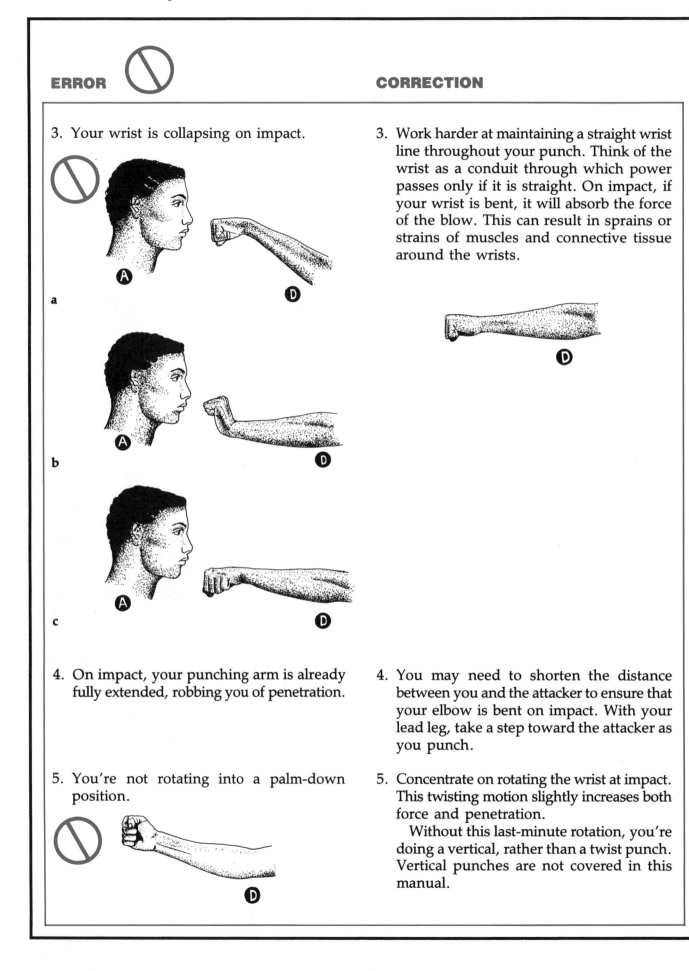

ERROR

CORRECTION

3. Your wrist is collapsing on impact.

a

b

c

3. Work harder at maintaining a straight wrist line throughout your punch. Think of the wrist as a conduit through which power passes only if it is straight. On impact, if your wrist is bent, it will absorb the force of the blow. This can result in sprains or strains of muscles and connective tissue around the wrists.

4. On impact, your punching arm is already fully extended, robbing you of penetration.

4. You may need to shorten the distance between you and the attacker to ensure that your elbow is bent on impact. With your lead leg, take a step toward the attacker as you punch.

5. You're not rotating into a palm-down position.

5. Concentrate on rotating the wrist at impact. This twisting motion slightly increases both force and penetration.

Without this last-minute rotation, you're doing a vertical, rather than a twist punch. Vertical punches are not covered in this manual.

ERROR	CORRECTION
6. You're jamming your fingers. 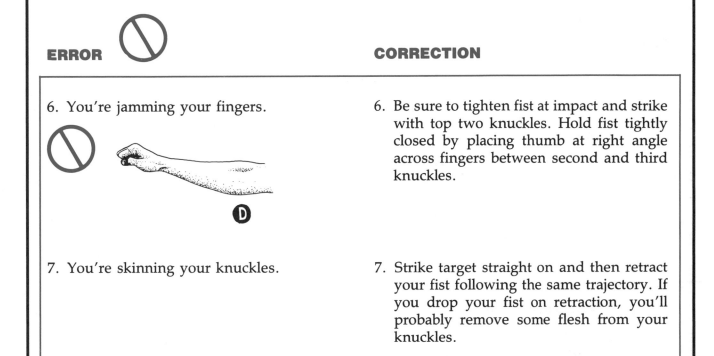	6. Be sure to tighten fist at impact and strike with top two knuckles. Hold fist tightly closed by placing thumb at right angle across fingers between second and third knuckles.
7. You're skinning your knuckles.	7. Strike target straight on and then retract your fist following the same trajectory. If you drop your fist on retraction, you'll probably remove some flesh from your knuckles.

HOW TO DO AN EYE GOUGE

An *eye gouge* is a front-facing strike thrown to one of the most vulnerable areas of the body. Given the great potential for inflicting serious damage, the eye gouge is generally used as a last resort. The defender must decide whether a given situation warrants such a drastic response.

Most assailants on the receiving end of this strike move immediately to protect themselves. They respond reflexively by closing their eyes, withdrawing their heads, and frequently trying to cover their eyes with their hands. This protective action may reduce the amount of damage inflicted by your gouge. Whatever the degree of injury, you've momentarily diverted the attention of the attacker from his or her assault on you. While he or she is distracted by his or her own pain, retreat to safety.

Keep in mind that premature or unsuccessful use of defensive strikes such as the eye gouge may anger your attacker and provoke a potentially more vicious response. Use this technique only when the situation warrants, and then with as much speed, accuracy, and force as is necessary to ensure that you have time to get away.

Begin by assuming a defensive stance.

Remember that although your practice stance is the ideal position from which to use this technique, an eye gouge can also be done while you're on the ground, pressed against a wall, or pinned to a couch. As with all hand strikes, it can be done with either your lead or trailing hand. Remember that there's relatively greater power in a trailing-hand technique because of the slightly greater trunk rotation used to launch the strike.

To do the strike, extend your hand toward the attacker's eyes following a slightly curved trajectory (see Figure 6.4). Your hand should be open and rounded, as if you were holding a large grapefruit. On impact, stiffen your hand and fingers into this position. Use your thumb and little finger to anchor the strike by digging them into the cheek or jaw of the attacker. Use the remaining fingers to press directly into the eyes. Penetrate as far as you can into the eye socket.

Note: Some will find it easier to press with only two fingers, rather than all three remaining fingers. Usually these are the index and middle fingers.

If possible, retreat immediately to safety. If retreat is not possible, quickly resume a defensive stance and guard. Prepare to follow up, if necessary, with additional strikes or blocks.

Figure 6.4 Keys to Success:
Eye Gouge

Preparation Phase

Lead Hand   **Trailing Hand**

_____ 1. Assume defensive stance _____
_____ 2. Eyes trained on attacker's eyes _____
_____ 3. Awareness of attacker's entire
          body   _____

Execution Phase

Lead Hand   **Trailing Hand**

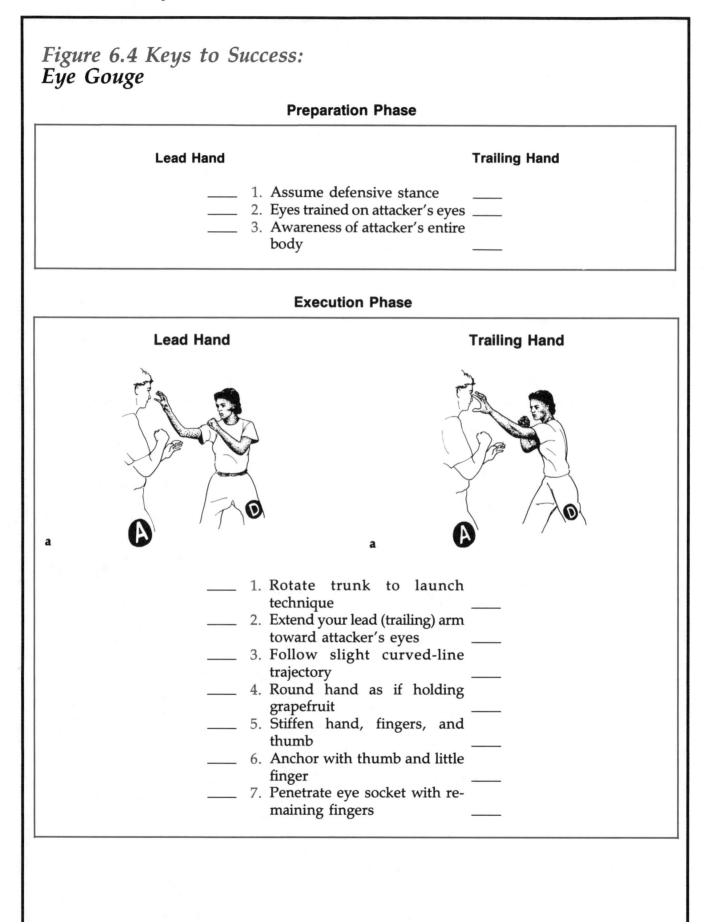

a   a

_____ 1. Rotate trunk to launch
          technique   _____
_____ 2. Extend your lead (trailing) arm
          toward attacker's eyes   _____
_____ 3. Follow slight curved-line
          trajectory   _____
_____ 4. Round hand as if holding
          grapefruit   _____
_____ 5. Stiffen hand, fingers, and
          thumb   _____
_____ 6. Anchor with thumb and little
          finger   _____
_____ 7. Penetrate eye socket with re-
          maining fingers   _____

Follow-Up Phase

Lead Hand		Trailing Hand
____	1. Retreat to safety	____
	2. If unable to retreat, then	
____	a. resume defensive stance	____
____	b. prepare to continue defense	____

Detecting Errors in an Eye Gouge

Errors with this technique are most often related to poor targeting and incorrect hand position.

ERROR ⊘

CORRECTION

1. You're extending with index and middle finger at the target.

1. You're doing what is called the "Three Stooges" technique. Round the entire hand. Stiffen (not straighten) your palm, fingers, and thumb in this rounded position.

2. Your fingers collapse on impact.

2. Keep fingers stiff to protect them as well as to maximize penetration.

HOW TO DO A PALM-HEEL STRIKE

This counterattack involves striking the nose or chin with the base of the palm. Because of the broader striking surface over which force is distributed, this technique packs a little less power than a punch to the same targets. On the other hand, that same broad striking surface makes it harder to miss the target, and reduces the chance of injury to your hand.

As with all other front-facing hand strikes, this can be done with either lead or trailing hand. Launch the movement with a sharp, short rotation of the trunk to generate maximum force. Once again, the more powerful palm heel is usually that of the trailing hand, due to the greater trunk rotation.

Begin by assuming what should be by now a very familiar defensive stance. To counter-attack, extend your arm in a straight line toward the nose or chin (see Figure 6.5). Hyperextend your wrist so that you're leading with the palm heel. Fingers are slightly curved and together and the thumb should be pressed against the side of the palm. The heel of the hand should impact the tip or bridge of the attacker's nose, or just underneath the chin. Push *through* the target. Retreat immediately, if possible. If you're unable to retreat, maintain a defensive posture and prepare to throw additional strikes.

Figure 6.5 Keys to Success: *Palm-Heel Strike*

Preparation Phase

Lead Hand   **Trailing Hand**

____ 1. Assume a defensive stance ____
____ 2. Eyes trained on attacker's eyes ____
____ 3. Awareness of attacker's entire body
                                                ____

Execution Phase

Lead Hand   **Trailing Hand**

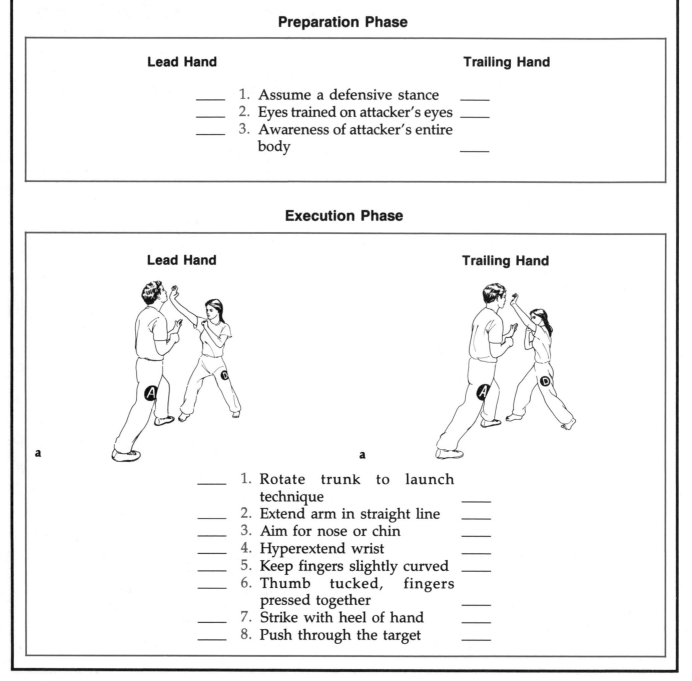

a   a

____ 1. Rotate trunk to launch technique
                                                ____
____ 2. Extend arm in straight line ____
____ 3. Aim for nose or chin ____
____ 4. Hyperextend wrist ____
____ 5. Keep fingers slightly curved ____
____ 6. Thumb tucked, fingers pressed together
                                                ____
____ 7. Strike with heel of hand ____
____ 8. Push through the target ____

Follow-Up Phase

Lead Hand		Trailing Hand
____	1. Retreat to safety	____
	2. If unable to retreat, then	
____	a. resume defensive stance	____
____	b. prepare to continue defense	____

Detecting Errors in a Palm-Heel Strike

Paying close attention to strike trajectory and hand position will eliminate most errors in a palm-heel strike.

ERROR

CORRECTION

1. Wrist is maintained in straight line on extension.

1. You're probably leading with fingertips and not the palm heel. Hyperextend your wrist to ensure that you impact with the palm heel and avoid jamming your fingers in the process.

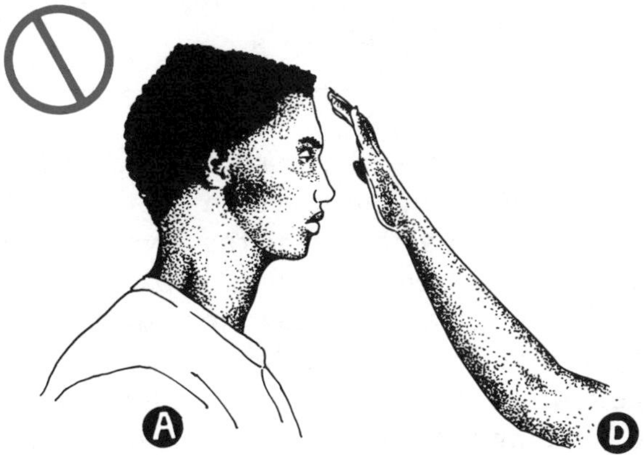

ERROR 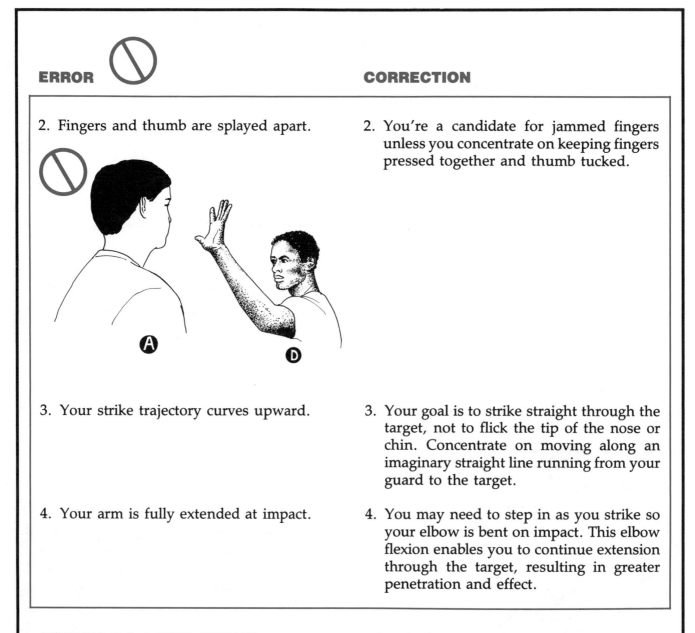 **CORRECTION**

2. Fingers and thumb are splayed apart.

2. You're a candidate for jammed fingers unless you concentrate on keeping fingers pressed together and thumb tucked.

Ⓐ   Ⓓ

3. Your strike trajectory curves upward.

3. Your goal is to strike straight through the target, not to flick the tip of the nose or chin. Concentrate on moving along an imaginary straight line running from your guard to the target.

4. Your arm is fully extended at impact.

4. You may need to step in as you strike so your elbow is bent on impact. This elbow flexion enables you to continue extension through the target, resulting in greater penetration and effect.

HOW TO DO A WEB STRIKE

This counterattack consists of a strike to the attacker's throat. Depending on the degree of force used, a web strike can elicit a gag reflex, cause discomfort, bruise, or possibly even collapse the windpipe. Because of the life-threatening damage that this strike can cause, it is considered potentially deadly force. As with all potentially deadly counterattacks, you must be able to justify use of this technique.

As noted in previous hand strikes, lead and trailing hands can be used to do the web strike. And, as already noted, trailing-hand strikes are somewhat more powerful because of the greater trunk rotation in launching the technique.

To do the web strike, assume a defensive stance then extend your arm in the direction of the attacker's throat at the level of the Adam's apple (see Figure 6.6). Separate your thumb as much as possible from your fingers. Fingers should be fully extended and locked together. Stiffen the entire hand to make the webbing between your thumb and index finger taut. It's this webbing that forms the striking surface for this counterattack. On impact, push through the target. Immediately retreat to safety, or, if necessary, resume a defensive posture and prepare to continue your defense.

Figure 6.6 Keys to Success:
Web Strike

Preparation Phase

Lead Hand   **Trailing Hand**

____   1. Assume a defensive stance   ____
____   2. Eyes trained on attacker's eyes   ____
____   3. Awareness of attacker's entire body
                                                                       ____

Execution Phase

Lead Hand   **Trailing Hand**

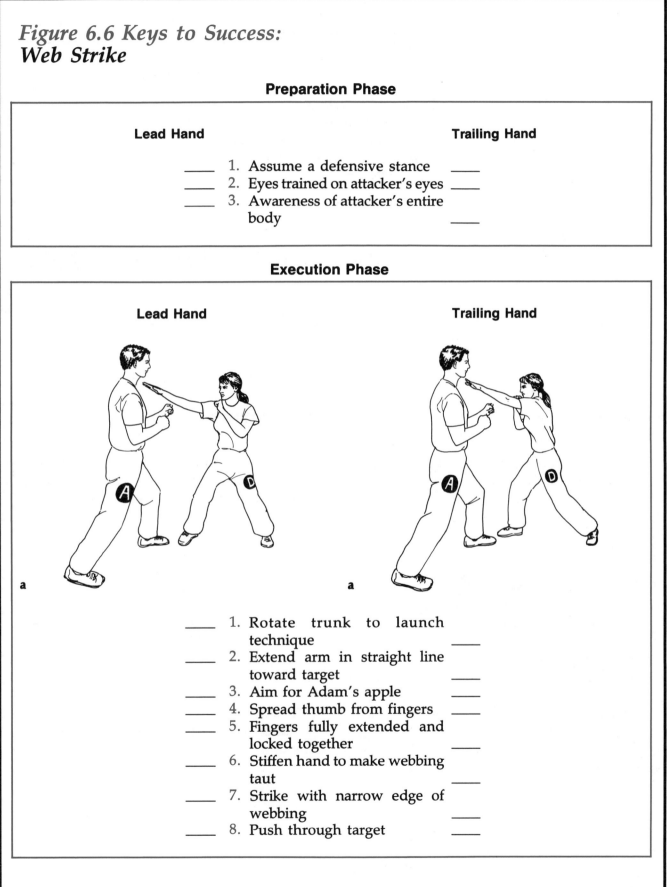

a   a

____   1. Rotate trunk to launch technique   ____
____   2. Extend arm in straight line toward target   ____
____   3. Aim for Adam's apple   ____
____   4. Spread thumb from fingers   ____
____   5. Fingers fully extended and locked together   ____
____   6. Stiffen hand to make webbing taut   ____
____   7. Strike with narrow edge of webbing   ____
____   8. Push through target   ____

Follow-Up Phase

Lead Hand		Trailing Hand
____	1. Retreat to safety	____
	2. If unable to retreat, then	
____	a. resume defensive stance	____
____	b. prepare to continue defense	____

Detecting Errors in a Web Strike

Having a broad enough spread between thumb and index finger and maintaining a rigid hand are the particular challenges of this technique.

ERROR 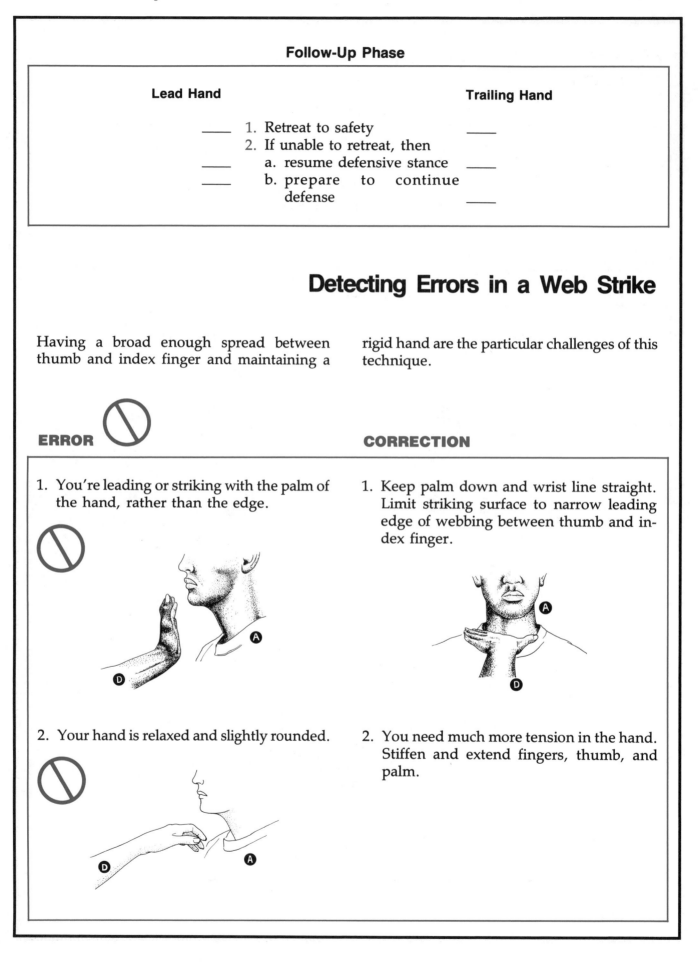 **CORRECTION**

1. You're leading or striking with the palm of the hand, rather than the edge.

1. Keep palm down and wrist line straight. Limit striking surface to narrow leading edge of webbing between thumb and index finger.

2. Your hand is relaxed and slightly rounded.

2. You need much more tension in the hand. Stiffen and extend fingers, thumb, and palm.

ERROR	CORRECTION
3. Your fingers are separated.	3. This is a setup for a jammed finger. Keep fingers locked together to protect them.
4. On impact, your elbow is locked.	4. You may need to step in as you strike to ensure that your elbow is bent on impact. This flexion allows continued extension through the target.

HOW TO DO A FRONT SNAP KICK

A *front snap kick* is generally directed at an attacker's knee or shin. Sufficiently powerful kicks to the knee may result in injury to the joint, including a fractured or dislocated kneecap.

Shin kicks can produce riveting pain (as anyone who's ever walked into a coffee table can attest), but are less likely to result in long-term injury to the attacker.

Kicks to small, peripheral targets, such as the knees or shins, require accuracy, precision, and balance. Whether you kick with your lead or trailing leg depends on the location and distance of the target.

From a defensive stance, lift your kicking leg into a *chambered position* (see Figure 6.7). Your thigh should be approximately parallel and your lower leg perpendicular to the ground. Remember to pull your toes back. Rapidly extend your lower leg toward the target and strike with the ball of your foot at the attacker's knee or shin. Be sure to hold your ankle tightly in flexion on impact. Drive through the target, then rechamber your kicking leg before setting your foot down.

Figure 6.7 Keys to Success: Front Snap Kick

Preparation Phase

Lead Leg		Trailing Leg
____	1. Assume a defensive stance	____
____	2. Eyes trained on attacker's eyes	____
____	3. Awareness of attacker's entire body	____

Execution Phase

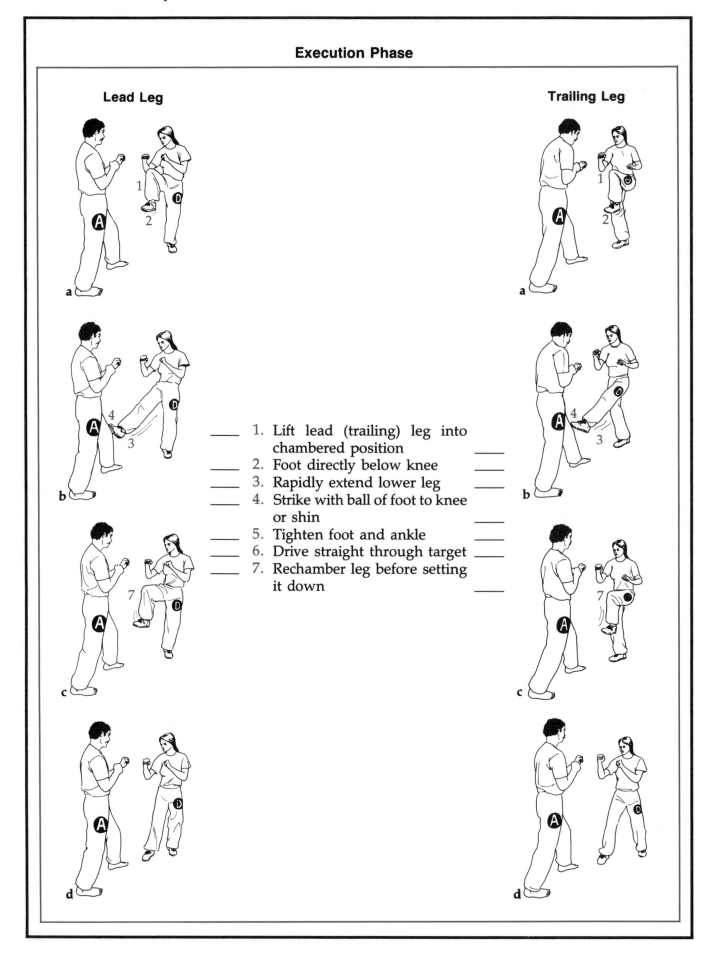

Lead Leg

Trailing Leg

_____ 1. Lift lead (trailing) leg into chambered position _____

_____ 2. Foot directly below knee _____

_____ 3. Rapidly extend lower leg _____

_____ 4. Strike with ball of foot to knee or shin _____

_____ 5. Tighten foot and ankle _____

_____ 6. Drive straight through target _____

_____ 7. Rechamber leg before setting it down _____

Follow-Up Phase

Lead Leg		Trailing Leg
____	1. Retreat to safety	____
	2. If unable to retreat, then	
____	a. resume defensive stance	____
____	b. prepare to continue defense	____

Detecting Errors in a Front Snap Kick

Omitting the initial chamber or rechamber and using incorrect foot and ankle positions are common beginner errors in execution of a front snap kick.

ERROR

CORRECTION

1. You're sweeping a straight leg up off the floor and toward the target (omitting initial chamber).

2. Your foot is dangling loosely at the end of your leg on impact.

3. Your toes are pointed, rather than pulled back.

4. You are dropping your kick following extension, rather than rechambering.

1. This means you're scraping across the target, rather than kicking through it. Practice doing only the initial chamber a few times to get the feel of it. This initial chamber enables you to use powerful extensor muscles for your front snap kick.

2. Tighten your foot and ankle at impact to stabilize them and provide a firm striking surface.

3. Toes must be pulled back to avoid jamming them. Make sure that the striking surface is the ball of the foot.

4. A rechamber helps you maintain balance after kicking. It also sets you up to do another kick.

Front-Facing Counterattack Drills

1. Mirror Drill

These solo drills enable you to begin to get a feel for these 5 counterattacks, without having to be overly concerned initially about accurate targeting.

Stand in front of a full-length mirror and assume a defensive stance. Moving at slow speed, alternate throwing lead and trailing punches toward your mirror image. Attend to all details of the execution phase.

Repeat with eye gouge, palm-heel strike, web strike, and front snap kick.

Success Goals =

  a. 30 punches

     15 correctly executed lead punches

     15 correctly executed reverse punches

  b. 30 eye gouges

     15 correctly executed gouges with lead hand

     15 correctly executed gouges with trailing hand

  c. 30 palm-heel strikes

     15 correctly executed lead-hand strikes

     15 correctly executed trailing-hand strikes

  d. 30 web strikes

     15 correctly executed lead-hand strikes

     15 correctly executed trailing-hand strikes

  e. 30 front snap kicks

     15 correctly executed lead-leg kicks

     15 correctly executed trailing-leg kicks

Your Score =

  a. (#)_____ lead punches

     (#)_____ reverse punches

  b. (#)_____ lead-hand eye gouges

     (#)_____ trailing-hand eye gouges

  c. (#)_____ lead-hand palm-heel strikes

     (#)_____ trailing-hand palm-heel strikes

  d. (#)_____ lead-hand web strikes

     (#)_____ trailing-hand web strikes

  e. (#)_____ lead-leg front snap kicks

     (#)_____ trailing-leg front snap kicks

2. Rocking Horse Drill

This partner drill helps you to develop accurate targeting.

Stand facing your partner in a defensive stance. Alternate throwing slow-speed punches toward each other. First one of you throws a punch, then the other, then the first again, then the other, and so on. Be sure to stop about 2 inches short of 1 of the 4 major targets for this technique (i.e., nose, chin, throat, or solar plexus). Also, make sure you're not doing all lead or trailing punches. Alternate the hand you use with each of your turns. The rhythm for this drill is slow and steady, back and forth, like a rocking horse.

Once you have each thrown 30 punches (15 lead and 15 reverse punches), switch to eye gouges.

When you've done 30 slow-speed eye gouges, switch to palm-heel strikes to the nose or chin. Repeat with web strikes and front snap kicks to their respective targets.

Practice each technique carefully and slowly. Aim for precise targets, but stop short of impact.

Success Goals =

    a. 30 slow-speed punches each to variable targets (15 lead/15 reverse)

    b. 30 eye gouges (15 lead/15 trailing)

    c. 30 palm-heel strikes (15/15)

    d. 30 web strikes (15/15)

    e. 30 front snap kicks (15/15)

Your Score =

    a. (#)_____ total punches

    b. (#)_____ total eye gouges

    c. (#)_____ total palm-heel strikes

    d. (#)_____ total web strikes

    e. (#)_____ total front snap kicks

3. Variable Front-Facing Strike Drill

Once again, assume a defensive stance, facing your partner. Alternate throwing slow-speed techniques as you did in the Rocking Horse Drill. This time, however, throw whichever of the 5 front-facing counterattacks you like. Try not to use the same technique on two consecutive turns. Vary your techniques and the hand or leg you use to throw them, in order to give them equal attention by the end of this drill. Concentrate on biomechanical detail and accurate targeting.

Success Goal = 3 minutes of continuous trading of front-facing strikes (stopping 2 inches short of actual targets)

Your Score = _____ 3 minutes completed (yes? or no?)

4. Kiyai Drill
(pronounced KĒ yā)

The power and speed of counterattacks is increased with the use of a sound we call a *kiyai*. Derived from martial arts, the term refers not only to a particular sound, but to ''the place where one's spirit meets one's voice.'' In other words, the kiyai is an expression of fighting spirit or determination to survive. This harsh, gutteral sound comes from the diaphragm, rather than the throat. Start out saying ''Hya'' in a normal tone. After a dozen or so repetitions, gradually increase the volume until the sound is one which would startle an attacker.

You'll notice that kiyaiing as you counterattack ensures that you're exhaling on the strike. This actually increases the force of the technique, while countering a common tendency to hold your breath while striking.

So the effects of a kiyai are multiple. It startles and disconcerts an attacker, draws others' attention to what is happening, increases the force and speed of your strikes by causing you to exhale on effort, and it often assists defenders in overcoming momentary shock and fear-induced paralysis.

After trying a few kiyais on your own, face your partner. Trade medium-speed techniques as in the previous drill. This time, kiyai each time you throw a front-facing counterattack.

Success Goal = 1 minute of continuous trading of front-facing strikes, each accompanied by a kiyai

Your Score = _____ 1 minute completed (yes? or no?)

5. Combination-Building Drill

In this drill, you'll develop combinations of front-facing counterattacks. In putting together a series of counterattacks, vary the limbs and targets. In other words, don't throw consecutive strikes to the same target or use the same body weapon. Some combinations will work better than others. For instance, a lead punch to the nose is frequently followed by a reverse punch to the throat or solar plexus. A kick to the shin will cause the attacker to drop the head slightly forward, making face targets more accessible. (The head always follows pain, that is, it moves toward whatever is hurting.)

Face your partner in a defensive stance. Moving at slow speed, throw 2 consecutive interlocking techniques. In other words, as you're retracting the first technique, launch the second. Have your partner throw a 2-strike combination. Alternate back and forth, rocking-horse fashion, throwing 2-strike combinations until they feel comfortable.

Now try 3-strike combinations, then 4 strikes, and so on until both of you have done 5 interlocking techniques in a row.

Use only those 5 strikes introduced in this step. Be sure to keep your centerline covered with the hand you're not using to strike.

Success Goals =

a. 30 seconds minimum of a variety of 2-strike combinations

b. 30 seconds minimum of 3-strike combinations

c. 30 seconds minimum of 4-strike combinations

d. 30 seconds minimum of 5-strike combinations

Your Score =

a. _____ 2-strike combinations completed (yes? or no?)

b. _____ 3-strike combinations completed (yes? or no?)

c. _____ 4-strike combinations completed (yes? or no?)

d. _____ 5-strike combinations completed (yes? or no?)

6. Block/Counterattack Drill

This drill combines an outside block with a front-facing counterattack. Assume a defensive stance with your left side leading, and face your partner (see Figure a). As your partner throws a slow right-handed punch toward your face, do a left outside block with your lead arm (see Figure b). Counterattack with a right punch (see Figure c). Do 20 repetitions, making sure you strike all of the punch targets (nose, chin, throat, and solar plexus). In the next 20 repetitions, substitute other front-facing counterattacks. Note that a kick counterattack is somewhat more awkward than hand strikes from this range.

Change leads and repeat the previous sequence, this time using right outside blocks and left counterattacks. Attacker will initiate each exchange with slow left-handed punches.

Note: Although you're practicing lead-hand blocking and trailing-hand counterattacks in this drill, it's also possible to do a trailing-hand block and a lead-hand counterattack. However, the pattern practiced in this drill is preferred, whenever possible.

a   b   c

Success Goals = In response to right-handed punch:

a. 20 left outside blocks followed by right punches to various punch targets (use left lead)

b. 20 left outside blocks followed by any of the 5 front-facing counterattacks, using right hand or foot (left lead)

In response to left-handed punch:

c. 20 right outside blocks followed by left punches to various punch targets (use right lead)

d. 20 right outside blocks followed by any of the 5 front-facing counterattacks using left hand or foot (right lead)

Your Score = In response to right-handed punches:

 a. (#)_____ block/punch counterattacks

 b. (#)_____ block/variable front-facing counterattacks

In response to left-handed punches:

 c. (#)_____ block/punch counterattacks

 d. (#)_____ block/variable front-facing counterattacks

7. Impact Drills

Once you've practiced strikes in the air, you can benefit from impact drills using hand-held foam shields or bags. The best bags to use are the commercial varieties available in many sporting goods stores. Some people make their own training aids by stuffing heavy duffel bags with rags or sand and hanging them from secure wall or ceiling holders.

The primary purpose of impact drills is to develop precise targeting and biomechanical proficiency. The shield or bag provides helpful (also occasionally painful) feedback on correct hand and foot position, trajectory, and targeting. It offers dramatic proof of the importance of aspects such as balance, alignment, and movement from larger to smaller muscle groups in generating maximum force with minimum effort.

To derive the greatest benefit and minimize injury, keep the following in mind as you practice these drills:

• Begin with very light impact. Gradually proceed to as much as 3/4 power and speed.

• Work for clear trajectories and precise points of contact. Avoid skidding on the bag surface to reduce skinned knuckles.

• Make sure you're using correct hand and foot positions in order to minimize the risk of jammed fingers, toes, wrists, and ankles on impact.

• Paint large Xs on your bags to help you develop more precise targeting.

• Position yourself in relation to the bag as you would be positioned relative to an attacker. Use good defensive stances.

• Don't do impact drills with techniques

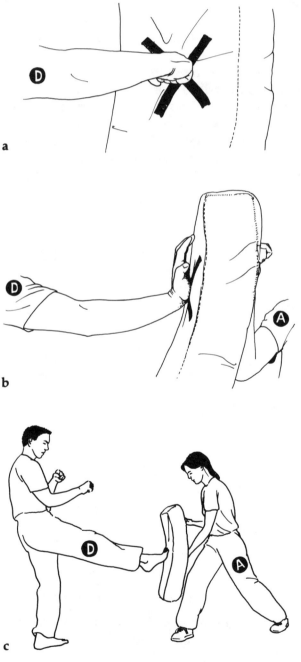

a

b

c

such as eye gouges and web strikes that have a high probability of jamming fingers. Of the front-facing strikes, punches (see Figure a), palm-heel strikes (see Figure b), and front snap kicks (see Figure c) are good candidates for impact drills.

Success Goals =

a. 20 correctly executed punches to bag (10 lead, 10 reverse punches)

b. 20 correctly executed palm-heel strikes to bag (10 lead, 10 trailing hand)

c. 20 correctly executed front snap kicks (10 lead, 10 trailing leg)

Your Score =

a. (#)_____ correctly executed punches to bag

b. (#)_____ correctly executed palm-heel strikes to bag

c. (#)_____ correctly executed front snap kicks to bag

Front-Facing Counterattacks Keys to Success Checklist

Have your teacher or a trained observer evaluate all of your front-facing counterattacks using the checklists within Figures 6.3 through 6.7. Bear in mind that the preparation phase and the follow-up phase are identical on all counterattacks. Be sure the observer evaluates you on both lead- and trailing-limb techniques.

Step 7   Rear-Directed Counterattacks

In this step you'll be learning those counterattacks typically thrown toward an attacker standing directly behind you. These include elbow jabs, head butts, back kicks, shin scrapes, and stomps to the instep.

WHY ARE REAR-DIRECTED COUNTERATTACKS IMPORTANT?

Many assaults involve being grabbed by surprise from behind. Given the decided disadvantage of being held from behind, it's important to know how to secure a quick release. The rear-directed counterattacks you'll learn are generally effective in doing just that. Notice that they utilize all of the body weapons and many of the body targets discussed in the previous step.

HOW TO DO AN ELBOW JAB AND HEAD BUTT

In response to an attack from behind, seek a broader base of support. Widen your stance, bend your knees, lower your center of gravity, and keep your back straight. Brace yourself from a forward fall by putting one foot further forward than the other. This is essentially the same as the defensive stance used previously, although this time you're facing away from your attacker.

To set up for an elbow jab, draw your striking arm out away from your trunk in a palm-up position. Place your arm at about a 45-degree angle to the front of your body. Slip your hips in the opposite direction from your striking arm in order to allow a clear, unimpeded, straight-line trajectory to the attacker standing directly behind you. To execute the jab, drive your elbow back into the attacker's floating ribs or solar plexus. The correct striking surface is the area just above the elbow point. This tough connective tissue is less fragile than the elbow tip. On impact, drive through the target area.

One effect of the elbow jab is to bring the assailant's head forward. (Remember: The head always moves toward pain.) It is for this reason that a head butt is an effective follow-up to the elbow jab. To do a head butt, hyperextend your neck and throw your head back as if to look straight up into the sky. If the attacker is approximately your height, the back of your skull should impact his or her nose. Because your skull is hard and able to absorb more force than the cartilage of the nose, this strike will be much more painful to the attacker than it is to you.

The elbow jab alone, or the elbow jab and head butt may cause the attacker to release you. In this case you should retreat immediately. If you fail to secure your release after using both of these techniques, continue throwing rear-directed counterattacks until the attacker releases any holds and backs off (see Figure 7.1).

Figure 7.1 Keys to Success: *Elbow Jab and Head Butt*

Preparation Phase

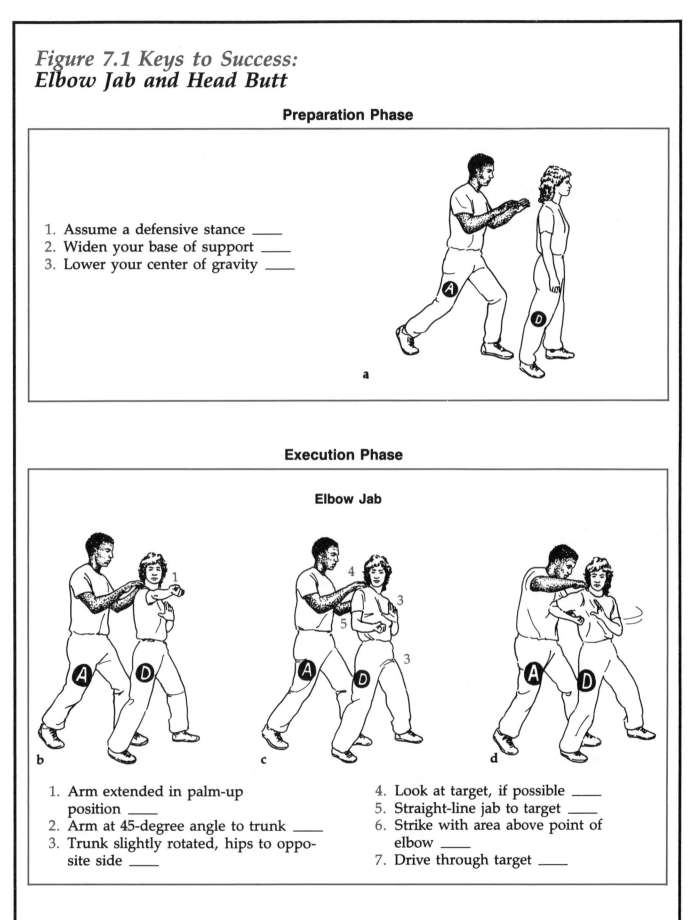

1. Assume a defensive stance ____
2. Widen your base of support ____
3. Lower your center of gravity ____

a

Execution Phase

Elbow Jab

b   c   d

1. Arm extended in palm-up position ____
2. Arm at 45-degree angle to trunk ____
3. Trunk slightly rotated, hips to opposite side ____

4. Look at target, if possible ____
5. Straight-line jab to target ____
6. Strike with area above point of elbow ____
7. Drive through target ____

Head Butt

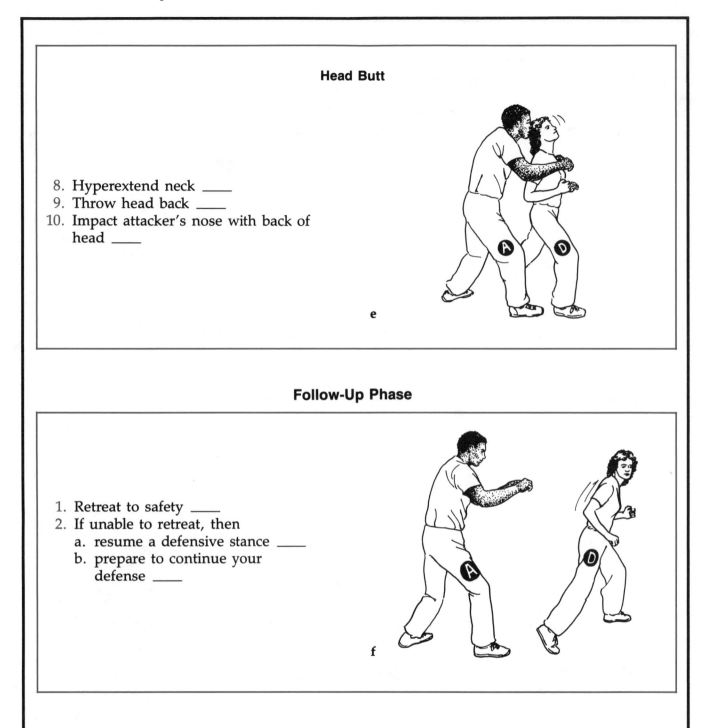

8. Hyperextend neck ____
9. Throw head back ____
10. Impact attacker's nose with back of head ____

e

Follow-Up Phase

1. Retreat to safety ____
2. If unable to retreat, then
   a. resume a defensive stance ____
   b. prepare to continue your defense ____

f

HOW TO BACK KICK, SCRAPE, AND STOMP

In addition to counterattacking with head and upper limbs, a defender can use lower limbs to respond to a rear attack. Used singly or in combination, a back kick to the knee, scrape of the shin, or heel-stomp on the instep are effective rear-directed counterattacks.

To back kick, lift your kicking leg into a chamber like the one used for a front snap kick. Turn your head and try to spot your target, usually the attacker's knee or shin. The heel of your kicking leg should be pointing at the attacker's knee or shin. Drive your leg and foot straight back and impact the target with your heel. Your ankle should be tightly flexed in order to avoid injury as you drive through the target.

If you're doing only a back kick, retract your leg along the same line as you extended it, and set it down. If you're continuing your defense, follow the leg extension with a scraping motion down the front of the attacker's shin using your heel or the blade edge of your foot. Finish the motion with a heel-stomp to the top of the attacker's instep (see Figure 7.2).

Figure 7.2 Keys to Success: Back Kick, Scrape, and Stomp Combination

Preparation Phase

1. Assume a defensive stance ____
2. Widen your base of support ____
3. Lower your center of gravity ____

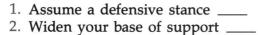

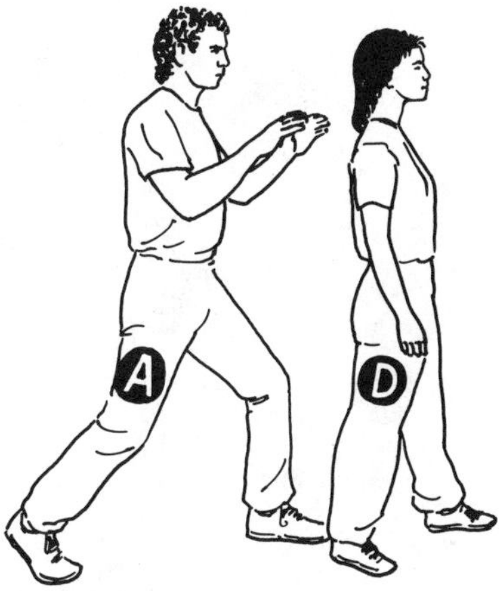

a

Execution Phase

Back Kick

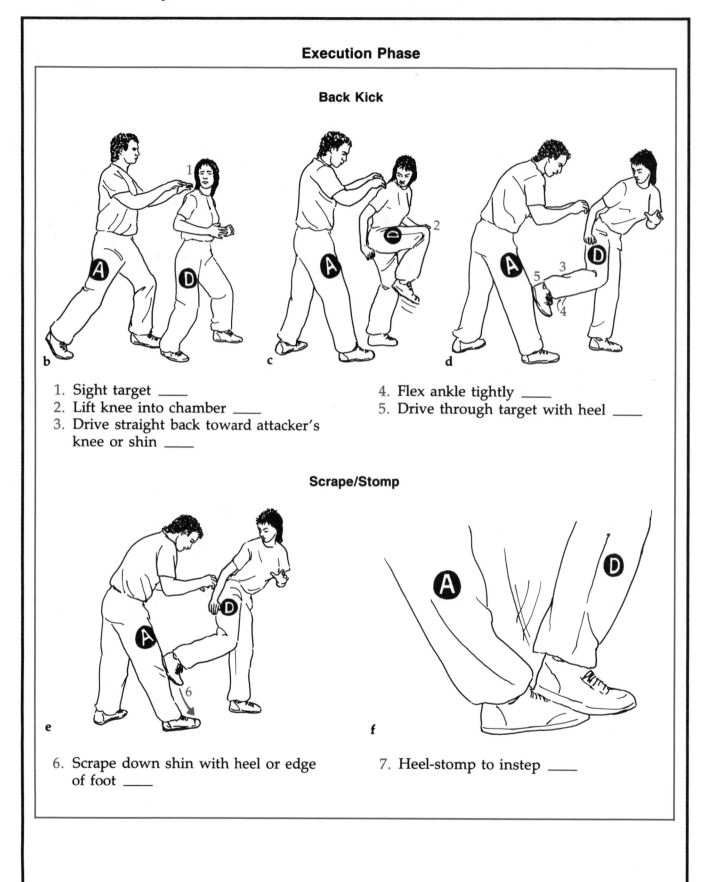

1. Sight target ____
2. Lift knee into chamber ____
3. Drive straight back toward attacker's knee or shin ____

4. Flex ankle tightly ____
5. Drive through target with heel ____

Scrape/Stomp

6. Scrape down shin with heel or edge of foot ____

7. Heel-stomp to instep ____

Follow-Up Phase

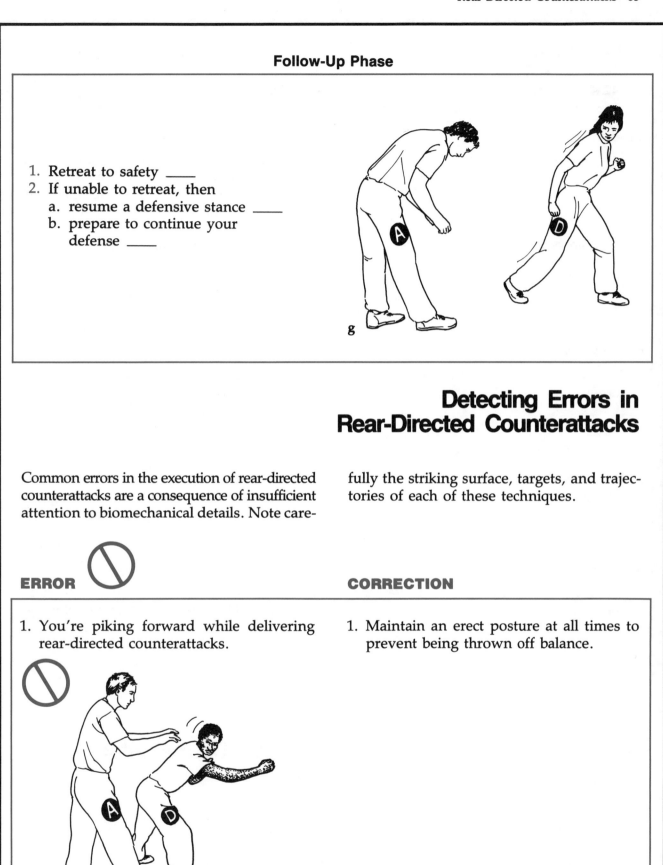

1. Retreat to safety ___
2. If unable to retreat, then
   a. resume a defensive stance ___
   b. prepare to continue your defense ___

g

Detecting Errors in Rear-Directed Counterattacks

Common errors in the execution of rear-directed counterattacks are a consequence of insufficient attention to biomechanical details. Note carefully the striking surface, targets, and trajectories of each of these techniques.

ERROR

CORRECTION

1. You're piking forward while delivering rear-directed counterattacks.

1. Maintain an erect posture at all times to prevent being thrown off balance.

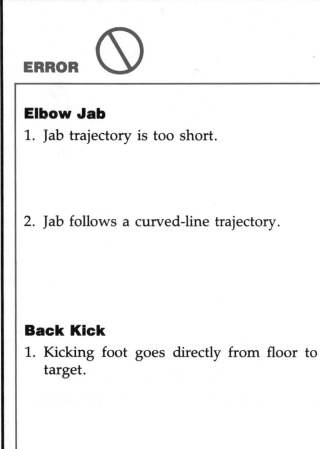

ERROR   **CORRECTION**

Elbow Jab

1. Jab trajectory is too short.

2. Jab follows a curved-line trajectory.

Back Kick

1. Kicking foot goes directly from floor to target.

2. Foot is dangling loosely on ankle at impact.

Stomp

1. Stomp is done with ball of foot on attacker's toes.

1. Be sure to extend arm out and away from trunk initially. This allows for a longer distance for the limb to travel to the target and build momentum.

2. Slip hips to the side and rotate trunk slightly to allow elbow jab to follow straight-line trajectory. Curved-line trajectory usually results from having to arc around your own trunk to get to the target.

1. This technique lacks necessary power. Do an initial chamber in order to line up foot for straight-line drive through target. A chamber also recruits powerful extensor muscles for a strong and effective kick.

2. This can easily lead to a jammed or sprained ankle. Ankle should be tightly flexed (toes pulled toward front of your shin).

1. Stomps are most effective when the heel is the striking surface and the target is the instep—the more fragile, bony arch of the foot.

Rear-Directed Counterattack Drills

1. Slow-Speed Solo Drill

Moving at slow speed, practice throwing the following rear-facing counterattacks to imaginary targets. Begin with 10 elbow jabs on each side for a total of 20 repetitions. Then do 20 back kicks only, taking care to rechamber before setting kicking leg back on ground. Finally, do 20 back kick/scrape/stomp combinations in slow speed to imaginary targets. During this last set, keep your spine erect to keep from losing your balance.

Work to develop a good feel for each technique, as well as balance and control in your delivery.

Success Goals =

    a. 20 correctly executed elbow jabs (10 each side)

    b. 20 correctly executed back kicks only (10 each side)

    c. 20 correctly executed back kick/scrape/stomp combinations (10 each side)

Your Score =

    a. (#)_____ correctly executed elbow jabs

    b. (#)_____ correctly executed back kicks only

    c. (#)_____ correctly executed back kick/scrape/stomp combinations

2. Targeting Drill With Partner

This drill presents an opportunity to develop the precise positioning and targeting necessary for throwing effective rear-directed counterattack combinations. For safety's sake, stop 1 inch short of your target on head butts, elbow jabs, kicks, and scrapes. Stomp off to the side of your partner's foot.

Have a partner stand directly behind you. Moving at slow speed, practice elbow jab plus head butt and then the back kick/scrape/stomp sequence. Then do a 5-technique combination by combining Drills 1 and 2, that is, elbow jab plus head butt plus back kick plus scrape plus stomp.

Success Goals =

    a. 20 correctly executed elbow jab + head butt combinations (10 on each side)

    b. 20 correctly executed back kick + scrape + stomp combinations (10 on each side)

    c. 10 correctly executed 5-technique combinations (5 on each side)

Your Score =

    a. (#)_____ correctly executed elbow jab + head butt combinations

    b. (#)_____ correctly executed back kick + scrape + stomp combinations

    c. (#)_____ correctly executed 5-technique combinations

3. Impact Drills

As with front-facing strikes, the accuracy of rear-directed counterattacks is improved by impact drills using bags and mat surfaces. Keep in mind the rules regarding impact drills:

- Begin with very light impact; don't exceed 3/4 force and speed.
- Work for clear trajectories and precise targeting.
- Use correct hand and foot positions to minimize jams.
- Position yourself in relation to the bag as you would be positioned relative to an attacker.

With these rules in mind, practice the elbow jabs (see Figure a) and the kick/scrape/stomp sequence (see Figure b). The elbow jabs can be practiced with bags or hand-held shields available through sporting goods and martial arts retail stores. The kick/scrape/stomp sequence can be done against a cushioned wall surface. Stand a regular tumbling mat on end and prop it against a wall. This provides just enough cushion to ensure that you can practice solid technique with minimal risk of foot injury.

For Success Goals c and d, tape or chalk Xs at various spots on your striking pad to challenge yourself with smaller targets. Determine a reasonable range of heights for elbow jabs to the solar plexus/rib area and back kicks to knees. Place Xs on 2 or 3 "ribs" and 2 or 3 "knees." Then, instead of being content with striking anywhere on your bag or shield, try for a direct hit on one of the Xs.

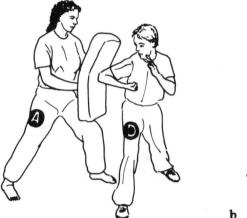 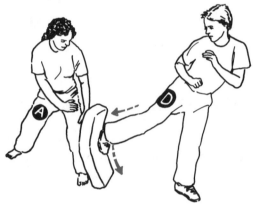

a   b

Success Goals =

   a. 20 elbow jabs into a bag or shield (10 on each side)

   b. 20 kick/scrape/stomp sequences into a cushioned wall surface (10 on each side)

   c. 18 to 20 elbow jabs impacting on an X

   d. 18 to 20 back kicks impacting on an X

Your Score =

   a. (#)_____ elbow jabs into bag

   b. (#)_____ kick/scrape/stomp sequences into cushioned wall surface

   c. (#)_____ elbow jabs delivered to X

   d. (#)_____ back kicks delivered to X

Rear-Directed Counterattacks Keys to Success Checklist

Have your teacher or a trained observer evaluate all of your rear-directed counterattacks according to the checklist items within Figures 7.1 and 7.2. Demonstrate them singly, then in combination with one another. Use elbow jab plus head butt, kick plus scrape plus stomp, and the 5-technique combinations presented in this step. Practice the techniques at no more than 3/4 speed and force. In addition to proper execution of each technique, work to improve balance and targeting.

Step 8   Side-Directed Counterattacks

In this step you'll learn two counterattacks that are effective against an attacker approaching from the side. One of these is a hand technique, called the *hammerfist*. The other is a kick, called a *side stomp kick*. Although either technique is effective by itself, the two can also be used in combination in situations requiring more than one strike.

WHY ARE SIDE-DIRECTED COUNTERATTACKS IMPORTANT?

Side-directed counterattacks enable a defender to respond quickly to an attack from either side of the body, without first having to turn to face the attacker. Turning into a front-facing position takes time and also increases exposure of the centerline. A more immediate and safer response is one done from a side stance—one in which you present the side, rather than the more vulnerable front of your body.

It's important to learn both a hand and a foot strike from this position, in the event that one of the lead limbs (i.e., either the arm or leg on the side presented to the attacker) is immobilized or injured.

HOW TO DO A HAMMERFIST AND SIDE STOMP KICK

A hammerfist is a strike that can be delivered on a horizontal plane or in a downward arc. The horizontal hammerfist is used for throwing to side targets, while the descending strike is used from a front-facing position. Here you'll learn only the horizontal hammerfist.

The preparatory position for this and other side-directed counterattacks is a side stance (see Figure 8.1). This is a wide-legged, stable stance in which the side of the defender's body is oriented toward the attacker. Feet are 1-1/2 shoulder-widths apart, knees are slightly bent, butt is tucked, back is straight, and the head is turned fully toward the attacker.

Arms are in a "side guard" position. Bend the lead arm at 90 to 120 degrees, and hold it vertically a few inches from the side of the body. This arm can be raised or lowered to protect the head or ribs. (Note that outside and inside blocks can be thrown easily from this guard.) The trailing arm shields the centerline as it cuts across the body. The fist, placed close to your lead elbow, affords additional protection to the ribs. Both hands are loosely fisted.

To do a horizontal hammerfist, let the fist of your lead hand drop forward until the forearm is nearly parallel to the ground. Then extend the arm toward the target, which is likely to be the attacker's nose, temple, jaw, throat, or neck. Just before impact, tighten your fist. The striking surface will be the little-finger side of the fist—a broad, well-cushioned surface. Strike through the target, as always, and then quickly return to the side guard position.

The *side stomp kick*, also delivered from a side stance, is generally directed at the front or side of an attacker's knee. Begin by lifting the kicking leg into a chamber, exactly like the one used in the front kick. Remember that both your hip and knee should be bent at approximately 90 degrees. For maximum power, launch this kick with a sharp thrust of the hip toward the side in the direction of the target. Extend your leg, leading with the heel and blade (outside) edge of your foot. When done with a tightly flexed ankle, this provides a firm and well-supported striking surface with which to impact your target. Drive through the target. Then rechamber your leg, that is, retract your leg along the same line it traveled during extension, and set it down. Throughout this kick, maintain a good side guard.

Figure 8.1 Keys to Success: Hammerfist and Side Stomp Kick

Preparation Phase

1. Assume a defensive stance ____
2. Side of body toward attacker ____
3. Feet 1-1/2 shoulder-widths apart ____
4. Knees slightly bent ____
5. Back straight ____
6. Lead arm bent at 90 degrees ____
7. Side of lead fist toward attacker ____
8. Trailing arm across centerline ____
9. Trailing fist protecting side of ribs ____
10. Hands loosely fisted ____
11. Head turned toward attacker ____

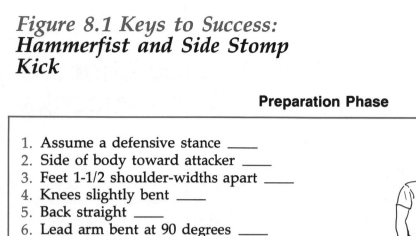

Execution Phase

Hammerfist

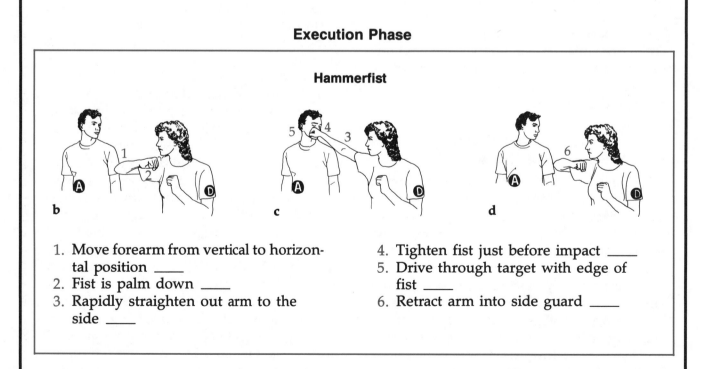

1. Move forearm from vertical to horizontal position ____
2. Fist is palm down ____
3. Rapidly straighten out arm to the side ____
4. Tighten fist just before impact ____
5. Drive through target with edge of fist ____
6. Retract arm into side guard ____

Side Stomp Kick

7. Lift leg into chamber ____
8. Commit hip, leg, and foot toward target ____
9. Foot travels along straight line ____
10. Heel and blade edge of foot lead ____

11. Foot at right angle to attacker's leg ____
12. Tighten ankle just before impact ____
13. Drive through target ____
14. Rechamber leg and set foot down ____

Follow-Up Phase

1. Retreat to safety ____
2. If unable to retreat, then
   a. return to a defensive side stance ____
   b. prepare to continue your defense ____

i

Detecting Errors in Side-Directed Counterattacks

The errors commonly associated with the hammerfist have to do with failing to maintain a straight wrist line or a tight fist. A lack of flexibility may make execution of a side-directed kick more challenging for some. If this is the case, practice more slowly and attend carefully to details of the setup and extension of the leg. A regular regimen of stretches will also help to increase flexibility.

ERROR

CORRECTION

Hammerfist

1. You're initiating the move with a straight arm, rather than a bent arm.

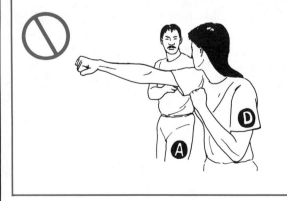

1. This could easily lead to an elbow sprain. Be sure to begin with a bent arm. Even at impact, there should be some elbow flexion.

ERROR ⊘   **CORRECTION**

Side Stomp Kick

1. You're leaving out the initial chamber and simply swinging an already straightened leg up toward your target.

2. You don't rechamber the leg—you drop the extended leg following impact with target.

3. Your foot dangles loosely at the ankle; your toes lead on extension.

1. This kick has no force. Remember to first lift your leg into a bent-knee position. Then straighten it out, driving downward in a straight line toward your target.

2. Retract your foot, retracing the line used for extension. The rechamber helps you maintain balance and prepares you for another kick.

3. You can easily jam toes or ankle this way. Pull the top of your foot toward your shin so that you're leading with your heel or blade edge.

Side-Directed Counterattack Drills

1. Rocking Horse Acceleration Drill

This partner drill is done standing side by side, with each of you assuming a side stance and guard. First you, then your partner throws a slow-speed hammerfist toward the other's face. (Remember that the precise target might be the nose, chin, jaw, temple, neck, or throat.) Be sure to stop at least 2 inches short of striking your target. As you continue trading hammerfists, gradually increase your speed. Go no faster than 3/4 of your maximum speed, or until you begin to lose accuracy and control. Once you've each thrown 30 hammerfists, face the opposite direction and repeat the drill with the other arm. Once you've practiced hammerfists on both sides, repeat the entire drill with side stomp kicks.

As you practice this drill, be sure to maintain the same range throughout the exchange of hammerfists, and then side stomp kicks. If you move in, you're likely to make contact with your target and possibly injure your practice partner.

Success Goals = 120 total counterattacks

a. 30 right hammerfists, ranging from slow to 3/4 maximum speed
b. 30 left hammerfists, ranging from slow to 3/4 maximum speed
c. 30 right side stomp kicks, ranging from slow to 3/4 maximum speed
d. 30 left side stomp kicks, ranging from slow to 3/4 maximum speed

Your Score =

   a. (#)_____ right hammerfists

   b. (#)_____ left hammerfists

   c. (#)_____ right side stomp kicks

   d. (#)_____ left side stomp kicks

2. Side-Directed Combination Drill

Put these two techniques together to form high-low and low-high patterns. Stand side by side with a partner, each of you assuming a side stance and guard. First one and then the other of you does hammerfist–side stomp kick combinations. Then each do side stomp kick–hammerfist combinations.

  Be sure to interlock techniques; in other words, while you retract the first technique of your combination, set up the second. Continue alternating these two patterns in a rocking-horse fashion, and gradually pick up speed.

Success Goals = 100 total combination counterattacks

   a. 25 right hammerfist–side stomp kick combinations

   b. 25 left hammerfist–side stomp kick combinations

   c. 25 right side stomp kick–hammerfist combinations

   d. 25 left side stomp kick–hammerfist combinations

Your Score =

   a. (#)_____ right hammerfist–side stomp kick combinations

   b. (#)_____ left hammerfist–side stomp kick combinations

   c. (#)_____ right side stomp kick–hammerfist combinations

   d. (#)_____ left side stomp kick–hammerfist combinations

3. Impact Drills

Your skill in both the hammerfist and side stomp kicks can be dramatically improved by practicing them on a bag or shield. Before doing this drill, review rules and suggestions presented in Step 7, Drill 3 regarding safe and effective use of bags and shields. Then try the hammerfist (see Figure a) and side stomp kicks (see Figure b) against a bag or shield. Practice 40 single side-directed counterattacks.

a

b

Success Goals =

a. 10 right hammerfists

b. 10 left hammerfists

c. 10 right side stomp kicks

d. 10 left side stomp kicks

Your Score =

a. (#)_____ right hammerfists

b. (#)_____ left hammerfists

c. (#)_____ right side stomp kicks

d. (#)_____ left side stomp kicks

Hammerfist and Side Stomp Kick Keys to Success Checklist

Have your teacher or a trained observer evaluate your performance of both of these techniques according to the checklist items within Figure 8.1. Do them singly, and in combination with each other, using the two combinations presented in this step.

Work for accurate setups, correct trajectories, and precise targeting with both counterattacks. Refer to the Keys to Success (Figure 8.1) to refresh your memory about biomechanical details of each one. Once you've perfected your execution, begin to work on speed and force of delivery.

Step 9 Response to Attempted Front Choke Hold

In this step you'll begin to apply the foundational skills learned in previous steps to a number of common *grab attacks*. A grab attack involves the sudden seizing of another person, or a part of his or her body, such as the wrist, arm, throat, or hair.

Being grabbed by the throat, whether from the front or from behind is one of the most frightening of grab attacks. In this step, you'll learn how to prevent the assailant you're facing from securing a choke hold. Then, in the next step, you'll learn how to respond when you haven't been able to prevent the hold from being secured and the attacker is strangling you.

WHY IS IT IMPORTANT TO KNOW HOW TO RESPOND TO AN ATTEMPTED FRONT CHOKE HOLD?

A *front choke attempt* is one of the most common of face-to-face attacks. It's also exceedingly frightening and dangerous. If the attacker succeeds in securing a stranglehold, loss of consciousness can result in as few as 4 to 14 seconds. This hold can put tremendous pressure on the carotid arteries, thereby blocking the flow of blood to the brain. It can also result in damage to the windpipe. Because of the potential for serious injury and even death to someone grabbed in this way, it's important to know how to prevent an attacker from securing this hold. The response that you'll learn is called a *flying wedge and push-away*.

HOW TO DO A FLYING WEDGE AND PUSH-AWAY

First, assume a defensive stance. Pay particular attention to those biomechanical details that make for a stable, grounded stance: wide base of support, lowered center of gravity, straight back, and one leg back to brace. Make sure your arms are in the guard position.

As the attacker reaches with both hands toward your throat, move your arms slightly forward and to the sides in an explosive movement. Just before impact, rotate your palms outward so that the striking surface is the little-finger edge of your wrist. Your forearms should still be nearly vertical so that interception will be at right angles to the attacker's arms. Intercept at the attacker's wrist (i.e., at the end of his power where you have greatest leverage) and move his or her arms to the sides. At this point your elbows should be bent at approximately right angles (the power angle for the elbow).

You've succeeded in deflecting the grab, and now you need to get out of range before your attacker attempts to grab you again. Immediately place the heels of your hands on the attacker's chest at points above the breasts and below the collarbones. Make sure your elbows are bent 90 degrees, your back is straight, and one leg is in front of the other. Quickly step forward with the lead foot, thrust arms out to full extension, and push the attacker away from you.

For maximum effect, both the flying wedge break and the push-away should be accompanied by a loud kiyai (see Figure 9.1). Also, an effective variation on the push-away is to step on the attacker's foot as you step forward. By pinning his or her foot while pressing the upper body backward, you can unbalance an attacker fairly easily.

Follow up by retreating to safety. As always, if retreat is not possible, assume your defensive stance and prepare to continue your defense.

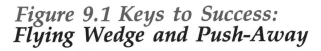

Figure 9.1 Keys to Success:
Flying Wedge and Push-Away

Preparation Phase

1. Assume defensive stance ____
2. Eyes trained on the attacker's eyes ____
3. Awareness of attacker's entire body ____

a

Execution Phase

Flying Wedge

1. Explosive movement of forearms forward and to sides ____
2. Forearms nearly vertical ____
3. Rotate towards palm-out position ____
4. Intercept at attacker's wrist ____
5. Strike with little-finger edge of your wrist ____
6. Move attacker's arms to the sides ____

b

Push-Away

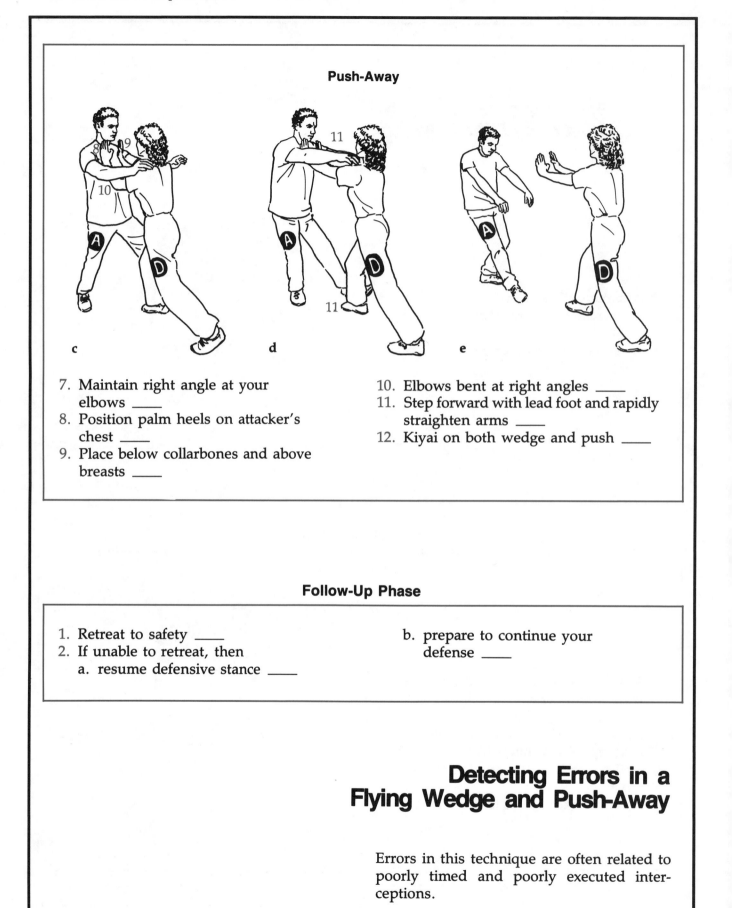

c   d   e

7. Maintain right angle at your elbows ____
8. Position palm heels on attacker's chest ____
9. Place below collarbones and above breasts ____

10. Elbows bent at right angles ____
11. Step forward with lead foot and rapidly straighten arms ____
12. Kiyai on both wedge and push ____

Follow-Up Phase

1. Retreat to safety ____
2. If unable to retreat, then
   a. resume defensive stance ____

b. prepare to continue your defense ____

Detecting Errors in a Flying Wedge and Push-Away

Errors in this technique are often related to poorly timed and poorly executed interceptions.

ERROR	CORRECTION
1. The attacker is able to secure a choke hold.	1. You're responding too late. Initiate the flying wedge the instant the attacker begins to move his or her hands toward your throat.
2. Point of interception is closer to your/the attacker's elbows than wrists.	2. Interception must be wrist to wrist for maximum leverage and effectiveness.
3. Your attacker is able to reverse your movement of his or her arms to the sides.	3. Maintain an angle of 90 to 120 degrees at your elbows for maximum holding power. Don't wait more than a second before following up with your push-away.
4. You're not getting much power on the push-away.	4. Keep your back straight. Place hands correctly on chest. Initiate push with arms bent at 90 degrees. Step and thrust in rapid succession. Keep your eyes and your intentions straight ahead.

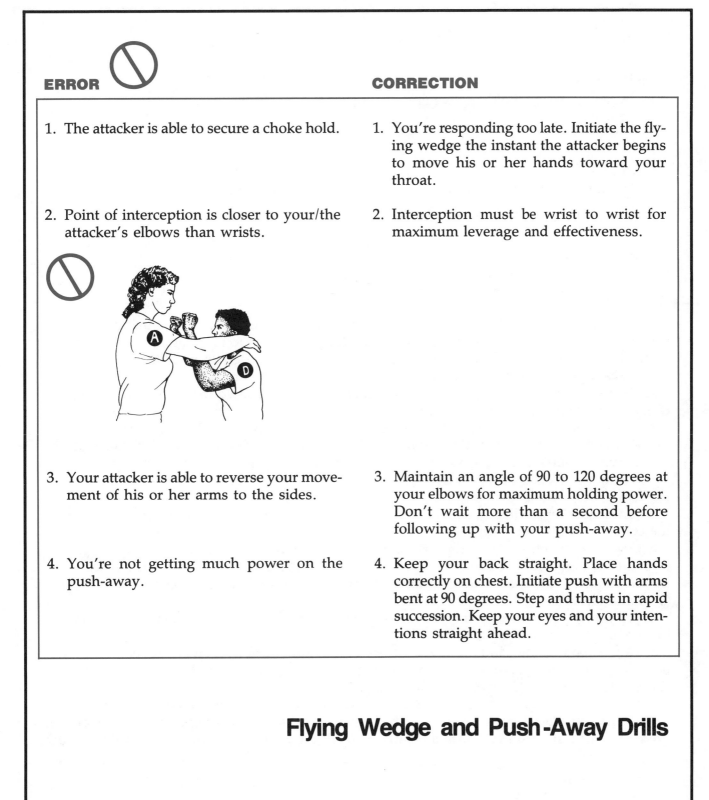

Flying Wedge and Push-Away Drills

1. Mirror Drill

Stand in front of a full-length mirror and assume a defensive stance. Do 25 repetitions of just the flying wedge, adding a kiyai to the last 10. Don't add the push-away at this time. As you practice, carefully monitor the details of your execution phase, including rotating the forearms into a palm-out position, maintaining right angles at your elbows, and moving explosively.

Success Goals =

a. 15 repetitions of the flying wedge without kiyai

b. 10 repetitions of flying wedge with kiyai

Your Score =

a. (#)_____ repetitions of the flying wedge without kiyai

b. (#)_____ repetitions of the flying wedge with kiyai

2. Progressive Partner Drill

The purpose of this drill is to develop your technique by practicing one component at a time with a partner. In addition to correct biomechanics, you'll need to focus on range and timing as you interact with an attacker. The challenge of remaining focused on your defense increases as the attacker adds shouts to rattle you and break your concentration.

a. Face each other and assume defensive stances. The designated defender will nod when ready for the attacker to reach for his or her throat.

Attackers should keep a number of things in mind during this drill. First, they must be sure to stand within easy reach of the defender's throat, that is, inside the critical distance zone. Second, they should keep fingers together and thumbs tucked to avoid accidental sprains and jams when defenders deflect their arms to the sides. Finally, attackers shouldn't fasten the insides of their wrists together when grabbing.

When an attacker reaches for the defender's throat, defender prevents him or her from securing the choke hold by executing a flying wedge.

b. Once you've completed 25 repetitions of the flying wedge, add the push-away. Don't rush through any part of the technique—take things one at a time. It's helpful to talk yourself through the technique by saying out loud, ''Grab,'' ''Wedge,'' ''Position'' (hands on chest), and ''Push'' (step and shove).

In practice, the push-away should be very slight in order to avoid possibly injuring your partner by shoving him or her to the floor.

c. Now speed up the drill a bit. As the attacker grabs (having received the nod from the defender), defender responds with rapid flying wedge, followed immediately by a controlled shove. Defender should kiyai on both the flying wedge and the push-away.

d. Same as c, although this time attacker shouts as she or he grabs in order to startle defender.

e. Finally, attacker decides when to grab. Be sure to pause between repetitions of the entire exercise. This last version enables defender to work on monitoring skills and reaction time.

Success Goals =

a. 25 flying wedges in response to attempted choke hold

b. 20 repetitions of flying wedge and push-away, talking your way through the technique

c. 15 repetitions of entire technique at a faster pace and with kiyais

d. 10 repetitions with attacker shouting

e. 5 repetitions with attacker determining when to grab

Your Score =

a. (#)_____ flying wedges only

b. (#)_____ flying wedges and push-aways with chanting

c. (#)_____ flying wedges and push-aways with kiyais

d. (#)_____ repetitions with attacker shouting

e. (#)_____ repetitions with attacker determining when to grab

3. Milling Drill With Flying Wedge

This drill was first introduced with the evasive sidestep. It's designed to add spontaneity and unpredictability to the attack, thereby enabling defenders to work on maintaining presence of mind and concentration.

A group of people (four or more) begin to mill rapidly about a room, taking care to keep two arm's lengths from each other. Periodically, one person points at another and shouts, "You!" Both freeze for an instant. The person who shouts, the attacker, then grabs for the defender's throat. Defender responds with a flying wedge. (Note: Don't add the push-away here, because it's too easy to shove people into each other in this drill.) Once the attack has been neutralized, both attacker and defender resume milling. Anyone can be attacker or defender. Remember that the person who shouts, "You!" is the attacker.

Success Goal = 2 minutes of milling, playing both attacker and defender roles

Your Score = (#)_____ minutes of milling

Flying Wedge and Push-Away Keys to Success Checklist

Have your teacher or training partner evaluate your response to an attempted front choke hold. Have them focus first on biomechanics of stance and execution using the checklist items in Figure 9.1. Then get feedback on timing (Are you reacting in plenty of time to prevent a choke hold from being secured?) and range (Are you close enough to execute the push-away without piking or straining to reach the attacker?). Work for balance, fluidity, and the ability to remain focused as the attacker adds various stressors to your practice of this skill.

Step 10 Response to Secured Front Choke Hold

This response applies previously learned skills to deal with a *secured,* as opposed to an *attempted, front choke hold.*

WHY IS A RESPONSE TO A SECURED FRONT CHOKE HOLD IMPORTANT?

In situations where you've not been able to prevent an attacker from securing this life-threatening hold, it's critical for you to gain your release immediately. You'll recall from the previous step that loss of consciousness may result in as little as 4 to 14 seconds after this hold has been secured.

A typical but frequently ineffectual response is to reach up and grab the attacker's wrists, and then try to pry or peel his or her hands from your throat.

Somewhat more effective is the flying wedge counterattack introduced in Step 9. If the defender can generate enough power, this response may break the attacker's hold. However, it may be necessary to first distract the attacker, usually by executing a painful strike to a vulnerable part of his or her body.

The defense in Figure 10.1 combines two of the front-facing counterattacks you learned earlier with the flying wedge. These counterattacks are the front snap kick and palm-heel strike introduced in Step 6.

HOW TO RESPOND TO A SECURED FRONT CHOKE HOLD

Assume a defensive stance. When the attacker grabs your throat, reach up immediately and grasp his or her wrists firmly. Give a quick yank on the attacker's wrists to relieve some of the pressure on your throat. Although this won't be effective in breaking the hold, it will help you maintain your balance as you do a front snap kick to the attacker's knee or shin.

Chamber your leg and kick hard and fast. Rechamber, then step down so that your feet are approximately shoulder-width apart. This ensures a solid base of support. While the attacker is momentarily stunned by the kick, use a flying wedge to break the hold on your throat. Finish with a palm-heel strike to the nose, then retreat to safety.

Figure 10.1 Keys to Success: *Response to a Secured Front Choke Hold*

Preparation Phase

1. Assume a defensive stance ____
2. Eyes trained on attacker's eyes ____
3. Awareness of attacker's entire body ____

Execution Phase

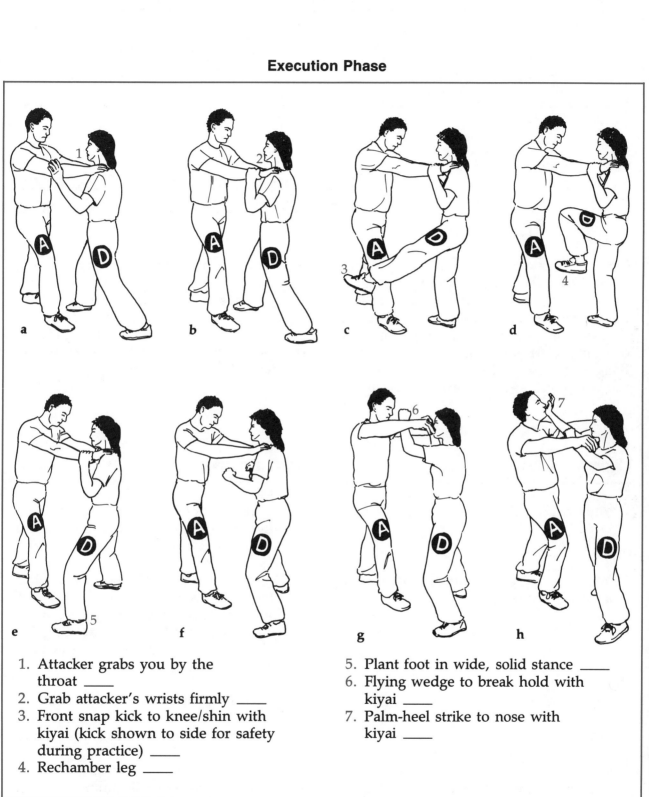

1. Attacker grabs you by the throat ___
2. Grab attacker's wrists firmly ___
3. Front snap kick to knee/shin with kiyai (kick shown to side for safety during practice) ___
4. Rechamber leg ___
5. Plant foot in wide, solid stance ___
6. Flying wedge to break hold with kiyai ___
7. Palm-heel strike to nose with kiyai ___

Follow-Up Phase

1. Retreat to safety ____
2. If unable to retreat, then
   a. resume defensive stance ____
   b. prepare to continue your defense ____

Detecting Errors in the Response to a Secured Front Choke Hold

The effectiveness of this defense is dependent upon each part being done correctly in order to set up for the next. An accurate and solidly delivered front snap kick distracts and makes the assailant pike forward, also causing a loosening of her or his grip. Then, a powerful flying wedge thrown from a solid base of support completes the break and opens up the attacker's centerline. Finally, a well-executed palm-heel strike rocks the attacker backwards and provides an opportunity for escape.

Give each component your full attention in order to ensure that you execute it properly and for maximum effect. Here are the most common errors at each point:

ERROR   **CORRECTION**

ERROR	CORRECTION
1. Your kick is missing the target.	1. Glance at your target before you kick to improve accuracy. Check keys to successful front snap kick in Step 6.
2. You're stepping down out of your kick into a high, narrow stance.	2. This will weaken your flying wedge, which is most effective when thrown from a wide, solid base of support. Step down into a wider, more stable stance, keeping feet 1-1/2 shoulder-widths apart, knees bent, center of gravity lowered.
3. You drop your guard after the flying wedge.	3. Return to a guard position immediately following the wedge. This positions your hands for a strike and protects your centerline.
4. Your strikes are missing their targets.	4. You may be rushing this multicomponent response. Concentrate on making one move at a time with power and accuracy.

Response to a Secured Front Choke Hold Drills

1. Building the Technique Drill

This drill breaks the response down into component parts and requires you to develop competence in each one before adding subsequent moves.

a. Begin by facing a partner and assuming a defensive stance. On the count of "One," the attacker grabs you firmly—not in the neck/throat region, but rather high on the shoulders to avoid injury or discomfort during practice (see Figure a).

Immediately grasp the attacker's wrists. On the count of "Two," throw a front snap kick and step down. To avoid injury to the attacker, throw your kick off to the side of the target (see Figure b). Repeat the sequence 15 times or until you're able to do it smoothly.

b. Now add a count of "Three." This is your cue to throw a flying wedge. Repeat this sequence of 3 counts at least 15 times or until you're able to move easily from the kick to the wedge break.

c. Then, add a count of "Four" to signal a palm-heel strike to the attacker's nose. Be sure to "pull" your strike, stopping 2 inches short of your target. Repeat the entire sequence 15 times or until each move is well executed.

d. Finally, on your nod, the attacker grabs. Move through the entire sequence fluidly and quickly, taking care not to fudge or rush any of the components. Add kiyais to the kick, the flying wedge, and the strike. Do 15 repetitions.

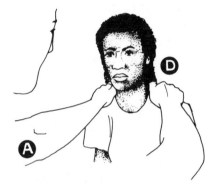

a

b

Success Goals =

a. 15 repetitions of the first 2 counts (grab on "one," kick on "two")

b. 15 repetitions of the first 3 counts (grab on "one," kick on "two," break on "three")

c. 15 repetitions of all 4 counts (grab on "one," kick on "two," break on "three," strike on "four")

d. 15 repetitions of entire sequence, working for fluidity and adding kiyais

Your Score =

a. (#)_____ repetitions of first 2 counts, by the count

b. (#)_____ repetitions of first 3 counts, by the count

c. (#)_____ repetitions of all 4 counts, by the count

d. (#)_____ fluid repetitions of entire sequence

2. Adding Stressors Drill

This drill involves adding a series of stressors, each designed to startle the defender. In this way, you develop your ability to overcome panic or disorientation and focus on the details of your defense.

a. Nod to attacker to begin attack. Attacker shouts "Shut up" or "Don't move" each time she or he grabs. Go through the entire sequence, with kiyais on each move.

b. Same as a, except that this time the attacker decides when to attack. Pause between each interaction to center yourselves and refocus.

c. This time, you, the defender, begin with eyes closed. Open your eyes the moment you're grabbed, and move deliberately into your response.

Starting with eyes closed dramatically increases the shock of the grab. Defenders are likely to fly into an ineffectual and panicky defense. This drill allows you to practice pausing for a split second, taking stock of the situation, and then moving deliberately into accurate and effective techniques.

Success Goals =

a. 10 repetitions with attacker shouting on grab

b. 10 repetitions with attacker determining when to attack

c. 10 repetitions of attacks initiated with defender's eyes closed

Your Score =

a. (#)_____ repetitions with attacker shouting

b. (#)_____ repetitions with attacker determining when to attack

c. (#)_____ repetitions of attacks initiated with defender's eyes closed

3. Variable Strike Drill

This drill is designed to help you develop greater flexibility of response and skill in building sequences of moves. In response to your nod, attacker secures a front choke hold. (Remember that attackers should grab the shoulder area, not the throat.)

Execute the front snap kick and the flying wedge. Now, however, substitute other front-facing strikes for the palm-heel strike. Do 10 repetitions of the entire technique, first substituting an eye gouge for the palm-heel strike. Then follow with 10 more repetitions, using a web strike. Do 10 more repetitions each, substituting a punch and then a push-away for the palm-heel strike. For the final 10 repetitions, do whichever of these front-facing counterattacks you like, or do a push-away. Work on executing techniques properly and accurately.

Success Goals =

a. 10 well-executed repetitions of sequence, substituting eye gouges for palm-heel strikes

b. 10 well-executed repetitions of sequence, substituting web strikes for palm-heel strikes

c. 10 well-executed repetitions of the sequence, substituting a punch to the nose, chin, or throat for the palm-heel strike

d. 10 well-executed repetitions of sequence, finishing with the push-away rather than a strike

e. 10 well-executed repetitions of the sequence, using palm-heel strikes, eye gouge, web strike, punch, or push-away as your final technique

Your Score =

a. (#)_____ repetitions using eye gouge for final strike

b. (#)_____ repetitions using web strike for final strike

c. (#)_____ repetitions using punch for final strike

d. (#)_____ repetitions using push-away instead of final strike

e. (#)_____ repetitions substituting technique of your choice for final strike

Response to a Secured Front Choke Hold Keys to Success Checklist

Have your teacher or an observer evaluate this response according to the checklist items in Figure 10.1. Have them pay particular attention to precise targeting of strikes and the general flow of one move to another. Work for balance, fluidity, and accuracy as you move through this multicomponent skill.

Step 11 Response to Mugger's Hold

In this and the next step, you'll learn responses to use when you're seized from behind. These incorporate several of the rear-directed counterattacks presented in Step 7. The first one is a defense used in response to a grab attack called a *mugger's hold*.

This grab is commonly done in one of two ways. In one version, the assailant places one arm across your throat while using the other hand to suppress a scream or to grip your upper arm (see Figure 11.1a). In the second version, the attacker uses his or her free hand to grip the wrist of the arm that is across your throat (see Figure 11.1b). This gives the assailant a more secure hold and increases pressure on the throat. Your response is essentially the same in either case, although the unsecured hold is easier to break. This defense consists of first relieving the pressure on your throat by rolling the attacker's arm down your chest while tucking your chin, then following up with appropriate rear-directed counterattacks, such as elbow jabs and back kicks.

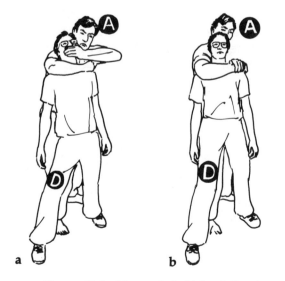

Figure 11.1 Mugger's hold (variations).

WHY IS A RESPONSE TO A MUGGER'S HOLD IMPORTANT?

Any attack from behind places you at a tactical disadvantage because you can't easily see or reach targets on the attacker's body. Of all the rear grab attacks, the mugger's hold is one of the most dangerous. In Figure 11.1, you can see how the attacker exerts pressure on the defender's throat with the forearm. This pressure can cause gagging and gasping and serious bruising, impair breathing, and in some cases, result in even more serious injury. It's essential to gain a quick release.

HOW TO RESPOND TO A MUGGER'S HOLD

When grabbed from behind, immediately assume the defensive stance. Widen your base of support and lower your center of gravity to provide greater stability.

Then, instantly reach up with both hands and grab the attacker's forearm and hand(s). Think of the forearm as a lever and make sure you grab either end. Place one of your hands just below the attacker's elbow. With the other, cover as much of the attacker's hand(s) as possible. (Keep in mind that if the attacker is using only one arm to maintain the hold, you'll be grabbing one hand. If the attacker is securing the hold with both hands, you'll be grabbing both.)

Raise both elbows in order to recruit powerful trunk muscles to help roll the attacker's arm down your chest. Roll the arm down and away from your neck so that the attacker's hand(s) end up in a palm-out position. Press the hands hard into your chest to increase torsion and discomfort at the wrist. The instant the attacker's forearm is off your throat, drop your chin to your chest. This ensures that the attacker won't have easy access to your throat again, if he or she rolls the arm back up.

Note: Defenders are often able to sense an attacker's approach from behind and take defensive action before contact is even made. They instantly drop the chin to protect the throat from the anticipated grab and in this way prevent attackers from securing a mugger's hold. Another option is to turn the chin toward the attacker's elbow to protect the air passage and reduce pressure on the throat.

Once you've rolled the attacker's arm off your throat, let go with one of your hands and prepare to throw an elbow jab to the solar plexus or the floating ribs. Use the elbow on the side toward which the attacker's center-line is oriented.

If the attacker's chest is flush with your back and neither side presents more accessible targets, let go at the elbow end of the forearm rather than the wrist. Then throw an elbow jab to that side. The attacker's ribs are most likely exposed on the same side as the arm used to grab. In addition, you have more control hanging on at the wrist than at the elbow. If you have a choice, let go at the elbow.

Once the elbow jab has distracted the attacker and loosened his or her grip, follow with a back kick to the knee or shin. Right elbow jabs are usually followed by right back kicks, and left elbow jabs by left back kicks.

The elbow jab alone may be sufficient to secure your release. Or both techniques may be required. It's also possible that you may have to do more than one of each technique. Repeat these techniques as many times as needed to break the hold (see Figure 11.2). Then quickly retreat to safety.

Figure 11.2 Keys to Success: Response to Mugger's Hold

Preparation Phase

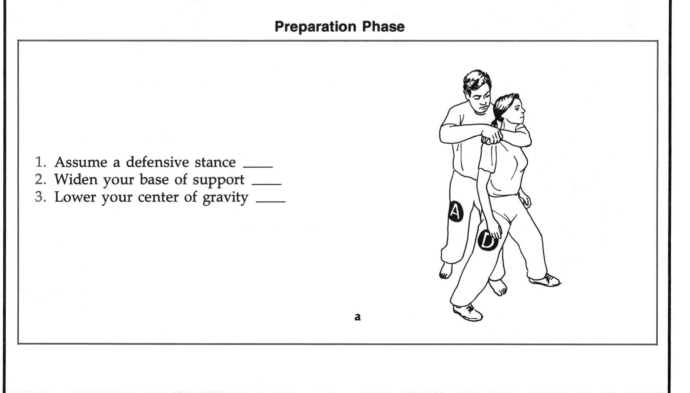

1. Assume a defensive stance ____
2. Widen your base of support ____
3. Lower your center of gravity ____

a

Execution Phase

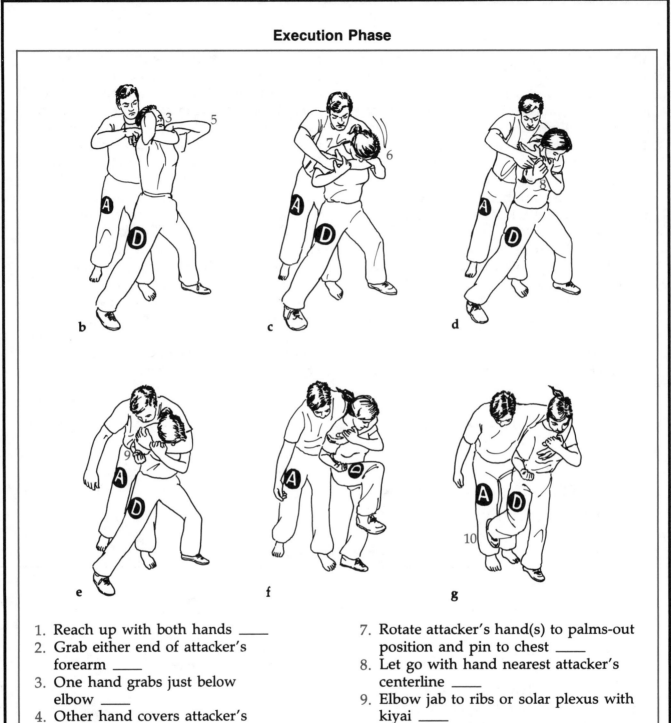

1. Reach up with both hands ____
2. Grab either end of attacker's forearm ____
3. One hand grabs just below elbow ____
4. Other hand covers attacker's hand(s) ____
5. Lift elbows ____
6. Roll attacker's forearm down and drop chin ____
7. Rotate attacker's hand(s) to palms-out position and pin to chest ____
8. Let go with hand nearest attacker's centerline ____
9. Elbow jab to ribs or solar plexus with kiyai ____
10. Back kick to knee or shin with kiyai ____

Follow-Up Phase

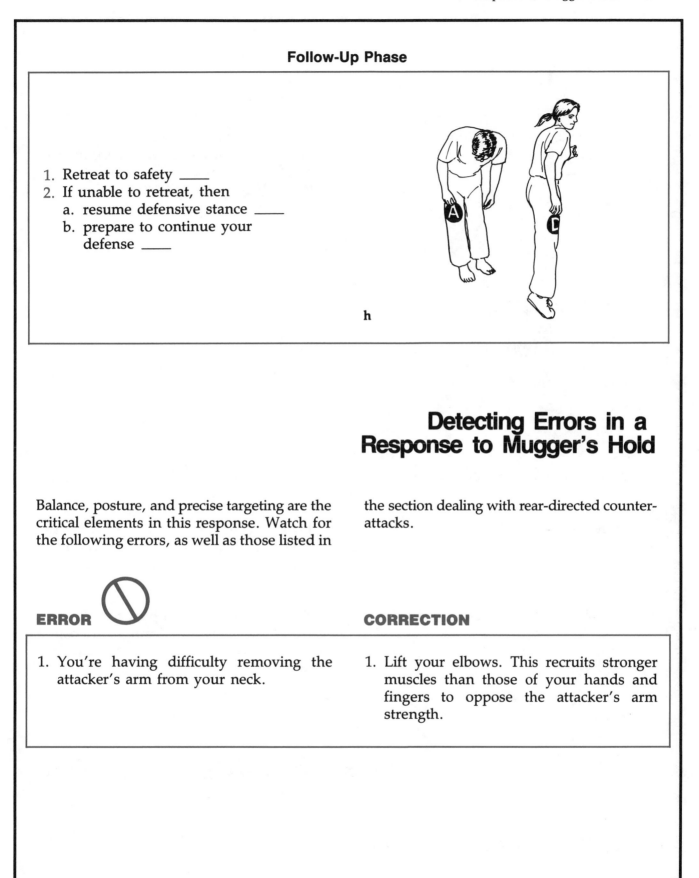

1. Retreat to safety _____
2. If unable to retreat, then
   a. resume defensive stance _____
   b. prepare to continue your defense _____

h

Detecting Errors in a Response to Mugger's Hold

Balance, posture, and precise targeting are the critical elements in this response. Watch for the following errors, as well as those listed in the section dealing with rear-directed counter-attacks.

ERROR	CORRECTION
1. You're having difficulty removing the attacker's arm from your neck.	1. Lift your elbows. This recruits stronger muscles than those of your hands and fingers to oppose the attacker's arm strength.

ERROR **ERROR**   **CORRECTION**

2. You're bending forward from the waist as you drop your chin.

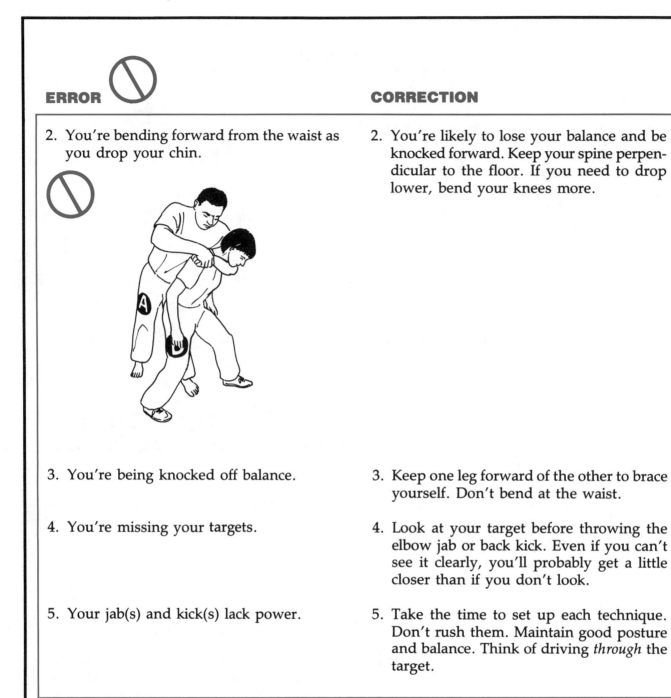

2. You're likely to lose your balance and be knocked forward. Keep your spine perpendicular to the floor. If you need to drop lower, bend your knees more.

3. You're being knocked off balance.

3. Keep one leg forward of the other to brace yourself. Don't bend at the waist.

4. You're missing your targets.

4. Look at your target before throwing the elbow jab or back kick. Even if you can't see it clearly, you'll probably get a little closer than if you don't look.

5. Your jab(s) and kick(s) lack power.

5. Take the time to set up each technique. Don't rush them. Maintain good posture and balance. Think of driving *through* the target.

Response to Mugger's Hold Drills

1. Building the Technique Drill

As in earlier steps, this drill breaks the response down into its component parts, and allows you to develop competence in each of these before adding subsequent moves.

a. Begin by having the designated attacker stand directly behind you. On the count of "One," the attacker secures a mugger's hold at the level of the Adam's apple, using one arm. Pressure on defender's throat should be kept extremely light. On count of "Two," grab the attacker's forearm at either end and roll it down the chest as you drop your chin. Be sure to rotate attacker's wrist and press it into your own chest for maximum control.

This sequence should be repeated 10 times or until you're consistently able to relieve the pressure on the throat with the attacker using only one arm to secure the hold. Then repeat the sequence 10 more times with attacker using his or her free hand to secure the pin. Note the increased difficulty of rolling the attacker's forearm from your throat, and the importance of lifting elbows to generate additional force.

b. Now add a count of "Three." This cues you to set up for an elbow jab. One arm is extended in a palm-up position and lined up with the target. The count of "Four" signals the jab to be released. The setup is given a count of its own to emphasize the importance of the preparatory position for maximizing force and establishing the correct trajectory. On the count of "Four," the elbow jab should be pulled, or stopped short of impact with the target. Repeat the first 4 counts 10 times or until the sequence is mastered. Then do 10 more repetitions, this time with the attacker securing the hold with his or her other hand.

c. Add count "Five." This signals you to lift the kicking leg into a chamber. This is preparation for count "Six," a back kick. The back kick should be directed at an imaginary target a few inches to the outside of the actual target. Repeat these 6 counts 10 times or until the sequence feels smooth. Then do 10 repetitions with the attacker securing the hold with his or her other hand.

d. Finally, on your verbal cue of "Now!" the attacker grabs. Move through the entire sequence smoothly and fluidly. You should add kiyais while executing the elbow jab and the back kick. Once this feels solid in response to an unsecured hold, try it with the attacker securing the hold with his or her other hand.

Success Goals =

a. 10 repetitions of the first 2 counts (grab on "One," roll it on "Two") with attacker's grabbing arm unsecured

   10 repetitions of first 2 counts with attacker's grabbing arm secured by the other

b. 10 repetitions of the first 4 counts (grab on "One," roll it on "Two," set up on "Three," jab on "Four") with attacker's grabbing arm unsecured

   10 repetitions of the first 4 counts with attacker's grabbing arm secured by the other

c. 10 repetitions of 6 counts (grab on "One," roll it on "Two," set up on "Three," jab on "Four," chamber on "Five," kick on "Six") with attacker's grabbing arm unsecured

   10 repetitions of 6 counts with attacker's grabbing arm secured by the other

d. 10 repetitions of entire sequence on defender's cue

   10 repetitions of entire sequence on defender's cue with attacker's grabbing arm secured

Your Score =

a. (#)_____ repetitions of first 2 counts

   (#)_____ repetitions with secured hold

b. (#)_____ repetitions of first 4 counts

   (#)_____ repetitions with secured hold

c. (#)_____ repetitions of 6 counts

(#)_____ repetitions with secured hold

d. (#)_____ repetitions of entire sequence in response to defender's cue

(#)_____ repetitions with secured hold

2. Adding Stressors Drill

In this drill, you'll once again add stressors to create greater realism. By adding to the challenge of doing this response in a practice drill, you can improve your recall under stress—your ability to recall appropriate defensive tactics despite alarm and surprise in actual situations.

a. Nod to the attacker to begin the attack. Attacker shouts "Shut up" or "Don't move" each time she or he grabs. Execute the entire defensive sequence with appropriate kiyais. Attacker may use a secured or unsecured hold.

b. Same as before, only this time the attacker decides when to attack. Pause a few seconds between each interaction.

c. Same as before, only this time you begin with your eyes closed. Open your eyes as soon as you're grabbed, and then execute this defensive response.

Success Goals =

a. 10 repetitions with attacker shouting with each grab

b. 10 repetitions with attacker determining when to attack

c. 10 repetitions of attacks initiated with defender's eyes closed

Your Score =

a. (#)_____ repetitions with attacker shouting

b. (#)_____ repetitions with attacker determining when to attack

c. (#)_____ repetitions of attacks initiated with defender's eyes closed

3. Moving Attack Drill

In this drill, both attacker and defender are mobile rather than stationary. With eyes open, begin to move slowly across the floor. The attacker runs up behind you and secures a mugger's hold. Go with this force until you're able to assume a solid, braced stance. Once you're stationary, execute the mugger's hold defensive response.

Note: The designated attacker in this drill should do a controlled grab, coming from behind with enough force to accelerate the defender's forward movement without knocking him or her down.

Success Goal = 8 out of 10 successful applications in response to moving attacks

Your Score = (#)_____ successful applications of technique in response to moving attacks

Response to Mugger's Hold
Keys to Success Checklist

Have your teacher or an observer use the checklist within Figure 11.2 to evaluate your response to a mugger's hold. Keep in mind key elements such as balance, posture, and precise targeting. Make sure you get feedback on your response to both variations of the mugger's hold.

Step 12 Response to Rear Bear Hug

Another common rear grab attack is the *bear hug*. In this attack, the assailant encircles your trunk with his or her arms from behind, pinning your arms to your sides in the process.

The response to the rear bear hug presented here involves the application of rear-directed counterattacks introduced in Step 7. Specifically, you'll practice the *back kick–scrape–stomp combination* and the *head butt* as a defense against this grab attack.

WHY IS A RESPONSE TO A REAR BEAR HUG IMPORTANT?

This common rear attack presents all of the tactical disadvantages of a mugger's hold, with an added and disconcerting twist. Two of your six body weapons—unfortunately, the two you depend on most—are immobilized. Presence of mind is essential in responding to this restrictive hold in which potential targets are sometimes tough to see. The defense presented here involves the precise and effective use of the remaining body weapons, the lower limbs and head, for throwing rear-directed counterattacks.

HOW TO RESPOND TO A REAR BEAR HUG

When grabbed from behind in a rear bear hug, you may be momentarily knocked off balance. As soon as you're able to regain your balance, determine the location of the attacker's knee.

Then lift your kicking leg into a chamber and drive it backward toward the target. Remember to keep your ankle tightly flexed and to impact with your heel. Without removing your foot, scrape down the shin with your heel or the blade edge of your foot. Finish with a heel-stomp to the attacker's instep.

This kick-scrape-stomp combination (see Figure 12.1) should bring your attacker's head forward, down closer toward the back of your head. To determine whether the attacker's nose or chin is within striking range for a head butt, you may be forced to rely more on tactile than visual feedback. If you sense that you can reach the target, throw your head back and strike with the back of your skull—a considerably less vulnerable surface than your attacker's nose or chin.

If the attacker releases his or her grip, retreat to safety. Otherwise, continue throwing rear-directed counterattacks until your attacker releases you.

Figure 12.1 Keys to Success: Response to Rear Bear Hug

Preparation Phase

1. Assume a defensive stance ____
2. Widen your base of support ____
3. Lower your center of gravity ____

Execution Phase

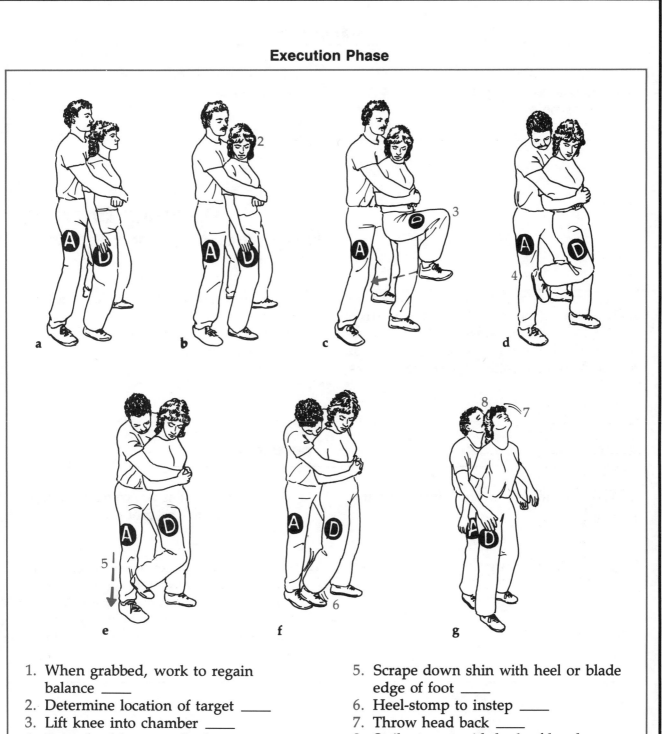

1. When grabbed, work to regain balance ____
2. Determine location of target ____
3. Lift knee into chamber ____
4. Drive heel into attacker's knee/shin ____
5. Scrape down shin with heel or blade edge of foot ____
6. Heel-stomp to instep ____
7. Throw head back ____
8. Strike target with back of head ____

Follow-Up Phase

1. Retreat to safety ____
2. If unable to retreat, then
   a. resume defensive stance ____

    b. prepare to continue your
       defense ____

Detecting Errors in Response to Rear Bear Hug

Because of the difficulty of seeing the attacker's body when grabbed from behind, most errors in this defensive response are related to inaccurate and imprecise targeting. Also, you may tend to rush multicomponent responses.

Concentrate fully on each technique and take it one move at a time. Finally, maintain an upright posture. Piking forward may cause you to lose your balance.

ERROR

CORRECTION

1. You're bending forward from the waist as you kick.

1. This is risky because you could be knocked forward and to the ground. Keep spine erect.

2. You're missing targets.

2. Take a second longer to set up your techniques. Sight your target before kicking, scraping, and stomping. Turn your head and look. Give each technique your complete attention before moving on to the next.

Response to Rear Bear Hug Drills

1. Slow-Speed Drill With Partner

Have your training partner grab you in a bear hug from behind. Very slowly, practice the entire response—kick-scrap-stomp combination, followed by a head butt. Make extremely light contact (called *whisper touch*) in order to avoid injuring your partner while still practicing precise targeting. Turn as much as possible and look at targets before delivering lower-limb strikes to ensure accurate placement.

Success Goal = 15 repetitions of the entire response using very light contact

Your Score = (#)_____ repetitions

2. Reverse Order and Flexible Response Drill

The purpose of this drill is to help you develop greater flexibility in the use of rear-directed counterattacks in response to a rear bear hug.

The first part of the drill is like Drill 1, except that the head butt precedes the kick-scrape-stomp. Practice this reverse order response to a bear hug until you're able to deliver it in a balanced, effective manner.

Then experiment with different 2-technique combinations, drawing from the 4 techniques used in response to a rear bear hug, such as head butt–heel-stomp combination; scrape-stomp combination; scrape–head butt combination, and so on. Note which combinations work well. In which does the second technique flow most easily from the first?

Success Goals =

a. 15 fluid repetitions of a head butt, followed by kick-scrape-stomp combination

b. 5 fluid repetitions each of at least 6 different 2-technique combinations (Under "Your Score," write out name of combination, for example, head butt–heel-stomp)

c. Identify the 2-technique combination that flows most easily

Your Score =

a. (#)_____ repetitions

b. (#)_____ repetitions of 1st combination _____

   (#)_____ repetitions of 2nd combination _____

   (#)_____ repetitions of 3rd combination _____

   (#)_____ repetitions of 4th combination _____

   (#)_____ repetitions of 5th combination _____

   (#)_____ repetitions of 6th combination _____

c. Circle the 2-technique combination that flows most easily

3. Grab-Bag Drill

By now you should be fairly proficient at executing singly the 5 different rear-directed counterattacks. These counterattacks, involving the use of all 6 body weapons, include head butt, elbow jabs, back kicks, scrapes, and heel stomps.

You know a couple of combination responses to 2 of the most common rear grab attacks. That is, you've applied specific combinations of the rear-directed counterattacks to 2 common rear grab attacks—mugger's hold and rear bear hug. You've also done some experimenting and improvising of your own, as in the previous drill.

In this drill, you'll be creating your own responses to 3 rear grab attacks not previously discussed in this book:

- Rear Choke Hold (see Figure a)
- Arm Bar (see Figure b)
- Double Wrist Grab (see Figure c)

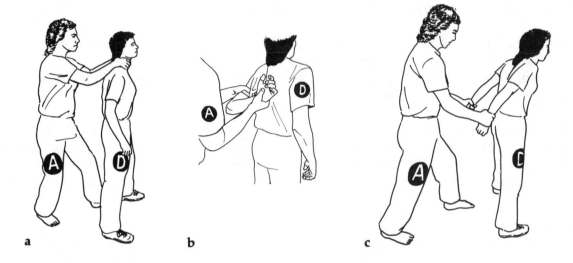

a   b   c

With each grab pictured, ask yourself which targets and body weapons are accessible. Drawing on skills you've already learned, decide which combination(s) of rear-directed counterattacks wuld be effective.

Experiment with a few different 2- and 3-technique combinations until you find one that flows. Then repeat that combination 5 times.

Remember that both you and your partner should move at slow speed and use whisper touch. Your partner should respond realistically to your strike by moving his or her head toward the point of impact. This makes it easier to determine which techniques might reasonably follow one another.

Have fun and be creative with this; improvise until the moves feel right.

Success Goals =

a. Identify possible 2- or 3-technique combinations in response to each of these 3 attacks

b. 5 repetitions of final choice

Your Score = Name combination of techniques and their respective targets, below

a. My 2- or 3-technique combination in response to rear choke hold:

1st technique _____ target _____

2nd technique _____ target _____

3rd technique _____ target _____

(#)_____ repetitions of best choice

b. My 2- or 3-technique combination in response to an arm bar:

1st technique _____ target _____

2nd technique _____ target _____

3rd technique _____ target _____

(#)_____ repetitions of best choice

c. My 2- or 3-technique combination in response to double wrist grab:

1st technique _____ target _____

2nd technique _____ target _____

3rd technique _____ target _____

(#)_____ repetitions of best choice

Response to Rear Bear Hug Keys to Success Checklist

Once again, have your teacher or practice partner use the checklist within Figure 12.1 to critique your response to this grab attack. This is an opportunity for you to perfect those rear-directed counterattacks executed with the lower limbs and the head. Have the observer pay particular attention to proper setup, targeting, balance, and ability to improvise responses to unfamiliar holds.

Step 13 Response to Wrist Grabs

Wrist releases, also called *quick releases*, are techniques for breaking free of wrist grabs. You'll learn three grab variations, including (a) a one-handed grab by an attacker to one of the defender's wrists, (b) a two-handed grab by the attacker of both of the defender's wrists, and (c) a two-handed grab by the attacker of one of the defender's wrists. These grabs are referred to as one-on-one, two-on-two, and two-on-one, respectively.

You'll also be practicing front- and side-directed counterattacks useful either as distraction techniques prior to the attempted wrist release, or as follow-up strikes to be executed once you've broken the hold.

WHY ARE WRIST RELEASES IMPORTANT?

Although being grabbed by the wrist(s) is less immediately life-threatening than other grabs, such as the choke holds you've been working with, it can still be intimidating. Wrist grabs are dangerous because you can be pulled or led by an assailant into more restrictive and risky positions.

HOW TO DO A WRIST RELEASE

There are two primary principles involved in a wrist release, regardless of the number of wrists grabbed or whether the assailant uses one or both hands. These principles are to (a) concentrate your force against the assailant's thumb(s), not fingers, and (b) maximize your power by incorporating trunk rotation and, when necessary, two-handed rather than one-handed releases.

In this step you'll learn two-handed releases, which assume the need for maximum force to break the hold. If you're able to break free and gain your release using only your trapped

hand, however, you shouldn't tie up the other hand unnecessarily. You should simply rely on trunk rotation and opposition to the thumb.

One-on-One Wrist Grab

If an attacker grabs one of your wrists with one hand, immediately fist your trapped hand. Cover it with your free hand, keeping both your wrists straight. Note the placement of the attacker's thumb. Move explosively against the thumb as if you intended to hyperextend it. As you oppose the thumb, use not only the power of both your arms, but your entire body by rotating sharply in the direction of the release.

Note that when the attacker uses a mirror-image grab, you can easily grasp your trapped hand with your free hand. The movement to oppose the thumb is then away from your centerline.

However, when the attacker's grabbing arm crosses his or her centerline (called a *cross-body grab*), this becomes a bit more difficult. You'll need to reach over the top of the attacker's hand to clasp your trapped hand, taking special care not to bend either of your wrists in the process. This time the movement to oppose the thumb is back across your own centerline.

The explosive movement against the attacker's thumb, whether done from a mirror-image or cross-body position, involves arcing over the attacker's forearm. It is because of this arc, slightly larger in response to a cross-body grab, that this technique is sometimes referred to as ''jumping the fence.'' Imagine that you're jumping from one side of the attacker's forearm (the ''fence'') over to the other, and in the process bending the thumb back.

Two-on-Two Wrist Grab

In this situation, the attacker uses both hands to grab both of your wrists. First, fist your hands and rotate both forearms inward so you can see your palms. Now place one fisted hand in the palm of the other hand. Assume a defensive stance with one foot back and sharply rotate your trunk toward your back foot. This rotation powers an explosive movement of your hands toward your rear shoulder. The combination of forces generated by the use of both arms and trunk rotation is considerable. When directed against the attacker's thumbs, which are already in a weakened position from the turning of your palms inward, this explosive move can often effect a release.

Two-on-One Wrist Grab

When the attacker uses both hands to grab one of your wrists, immediately fist your trapped hand. Reach between the attacker's forearms to clasp your fisted hand with your free hand. Take a defensive stance with one leg back and then powerfully rotate your trunk in the direction of your rear leg. Simultaneously pull your hands toward your rear shoulder, focusing considerable force against the attacker's thumbs, which are the weak link of his or her grip.

PRELIMINARY MOVES AND FOLLOW-UPS

There are a number of preliminary moves that increase the likelihood of success in wrist releases. One of these involves the use of a painful distraction just prior to the attempted release, usually a sharp kick to the attacker's shins. When the attacker's focus is split by the effects of the kick, he or she is less likely to resist your efforts to gain your release. These *distraction techniques* are explained in the Split-Focus Drill (Drill 2).

A more subtle (and considerably less painful) preliminary move involves completely relaxing the arm being grabbed by the attacker, as if to suggest compliance or docility. Although this response may run counter to your impulses, the unexpected lack of resistance frequently causes an attacker to relax his or her grip. When this happens, react instantly with an explosive release.

Once you've secured your release, it's sometimes necessary to follow up with a counterattack. The purpose of this follow-up strike or kick is to discourage the attacker from attempting another hold, or pressing the assault in any other way. Follow-ups are explored in Drill 3.

The wrist releases for breaking free of three wrist grabs are shown in Figure 13.1.

Figure 13.1 Keys to Success: *Wrist Releases*

Preparation Phase

1. Assume a defensive stance ____
2. Eyes trained on attacker's eyes ____
3. Awareness of attacker's entire body ____

Execution Phase

1-on-1 Wrist Grab

Mirror-image grab   *Cross-body grab*

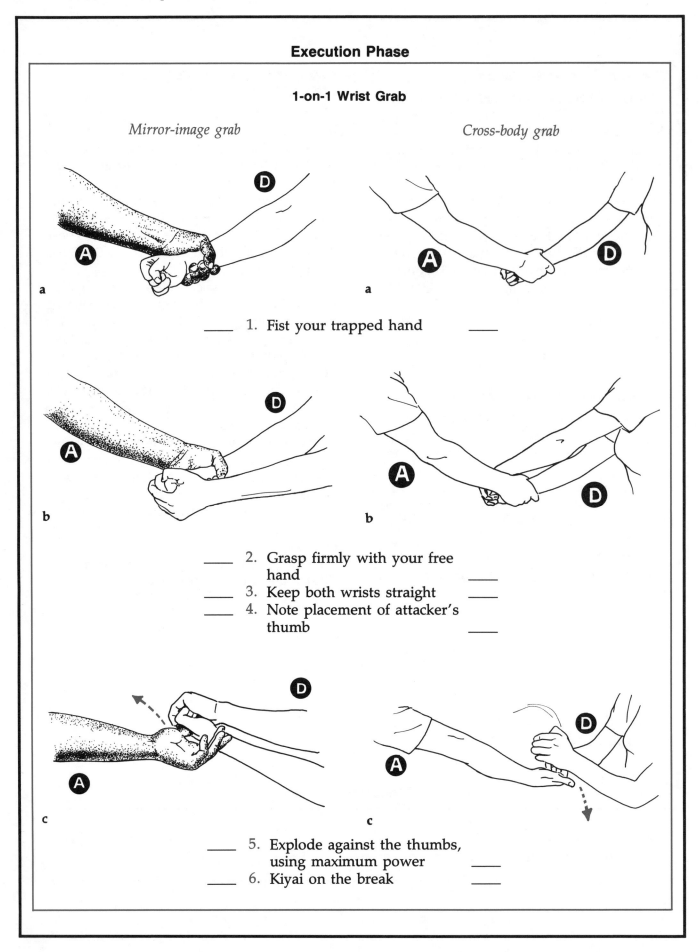

a   a

____ 1. Fist your trapped hand   ____

b   b

____ 2. Grasp firmly with your free
hand   ____
____ 3. Keep both wrists straight   ____
____ 4. Note placement of attacker's
thumb   ____

c   c

____ 5. Explode against the thumbs,
using maximum power   ____
____ 6. Kiyai on the break   ____

2-on-2 Wrist Grab

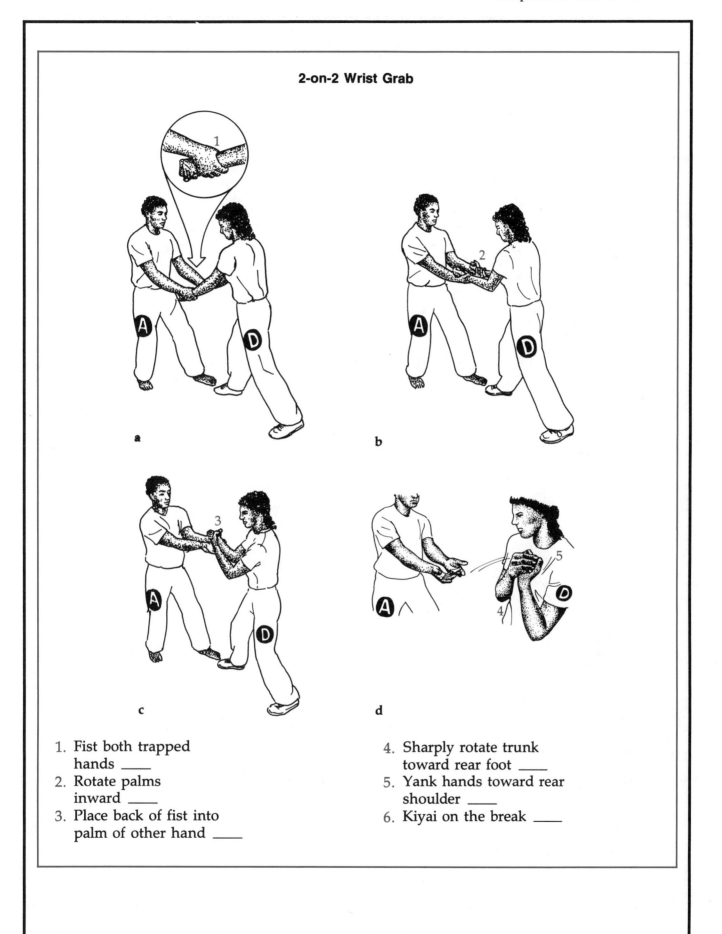

1. Fist both trapped hands ____
2. Rotate palms inward ____
3. Place back of fist into palm of other hand ____
4. Sharply rotate trunk toward rear foot ____
5. Yank hands toward rear shoulder ____
6. Kiyai on the break ____

2-on-1 Wrist Grab

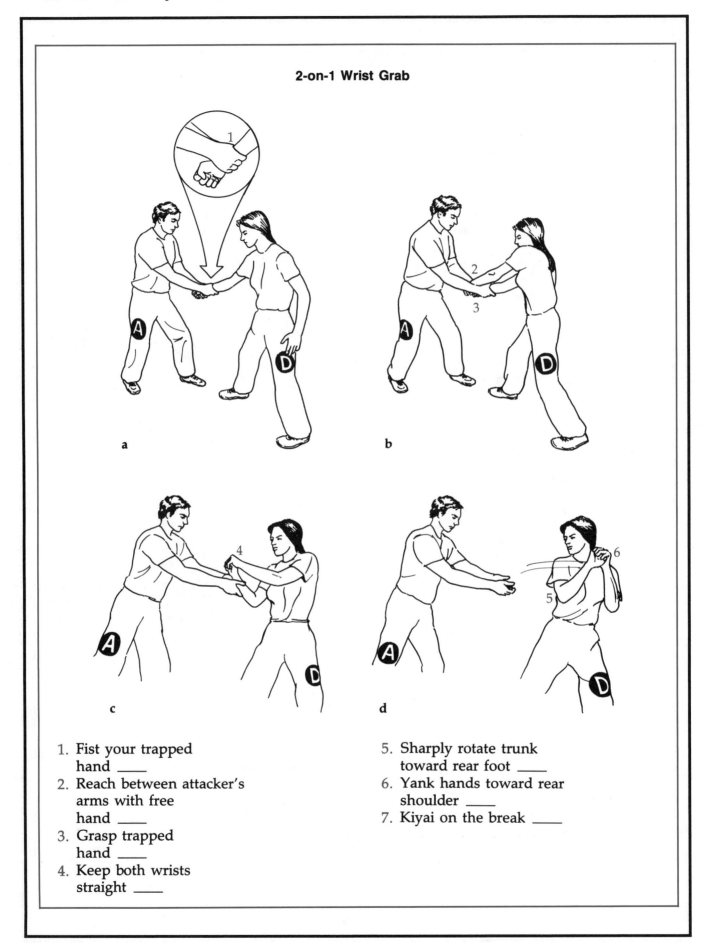

a

b

c

d

1. Fist your trapped hand ____
2. Reach between attacker's arms with free hand ____
3. Grasp trapped hand ____
4. Keep both wrists straight ____
5. Sharply rotate trunk toward rear foot ____
6. Yank hands toward rear shoulder ____
7. Kiyai on the break ____

Follow-Up Phase

1. Retreat to safety ____
2. If unable to retreat, then
   a. resume defensive
      stance ____

   b. prepare to continue
      your defense ____

Detecting Errors in Wrist Releases

A common error in wrist releases is a lack of trunk rotation to power the break. This leaves you entirely dependent on the strength of your arms alone to effect a release. Other errors are related to improper grip, bent wrists, and opposing the attacker's fingers rather than thumb(s).

ERROR

CORRECTION

1. You're bending your wrists on your release attempts.

1. A bent wrist line weakens your effort and increases your risk of a sprain. Concentrate on keeping wrists straight. Try temporarily splinting them with a ruler or tongue depressor maintaining a straight wrist line.

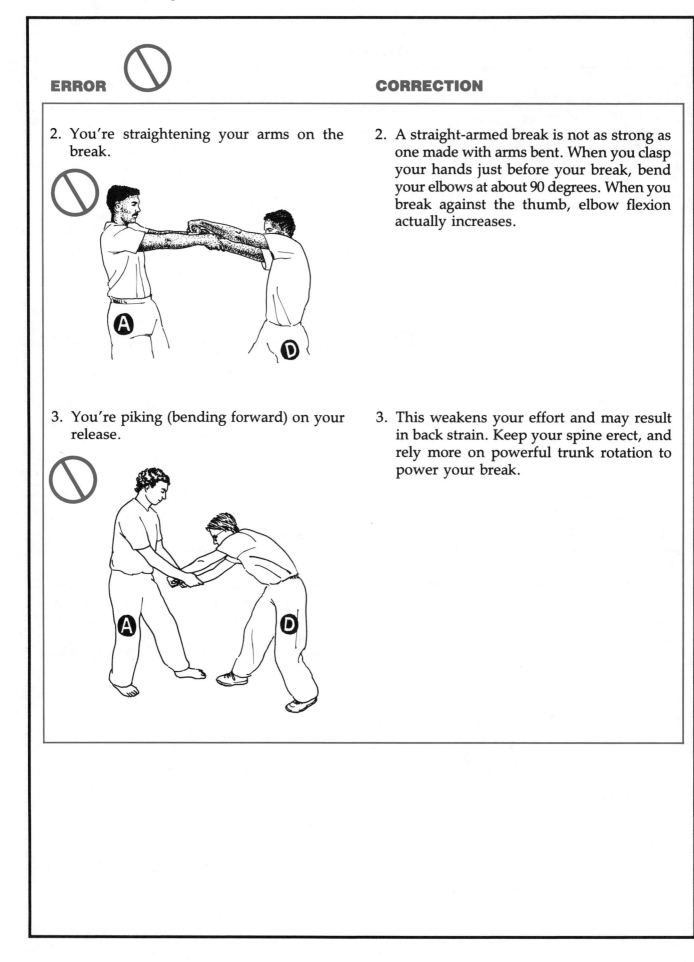

ERROR

CORRECTION

2. You're straightening your arms on the break.

2. A straight-armed break is not as strong as one made with arms bent. When you clasp your hands just before your break, bend your elbows at about 90 degrees. When you break against the thumb, elbow flexion actually increases.

3. You're piking (bending forward) on your release.

3. This weakens your effort and may result in back strain. Keep your spine erect, and rely more on powerful trunk rotation to power your break.

ERROR

CORRECTION

4. On 2-on-2 and 2-on-1 grabs, you're bringing your freed hands to your lead shoulder.

4. This move restricts the degree of trunk rotation (and consequently your power) and also causes you to twist your spine uncomfortably. Bring freed hands to your rear shoulder (i.e., the same direction as your back foot).

5. You're lacing your fingers together instead of covering one fist with the other.

5. Fingers can be easily crushed and injured in this position. A safer and more effective grip is to completely cover one of your fists with your other hand. This enables you to combine power while protecting your fingers.

Wrist-Release Drills

1. Quick-Release Drill

This partner drill is designed to help you increase the quickness of your response to the three wrist-grab variations. In response to each grab, quickly determine the location of the thumb, identify the appropriate release trajectory, and execute the break. This process should become increasingly spontaneous with practice, requiring less and less "think" time before the break.

Throughout these drills, attackers should use a light grip so defenders can concentrate on form and speed rather than power. Using a light grip spares the wrists during high repetition drills such as these.

First, ask your partner to grab you 1-on-1, using both cross-body and mirror-image grabs. With each successive grab, try to respond more quickly than the time before. Repeat until your releases are explosive and immediate. Repeat with 2-on-2 and 2-on-1 grabs, respectively. Finally, challenge yourself further with a random-order drill in which your partner uses any one of the three grabs. Respond with the appropriate release, all the while working toward more explosive and immediate breaks.

Success Goals =

   a. 13 out of 15 correctly executed wrist releases in response to 1-on-1 wrist grabs

   b. 13 out of 15 correctly executed wrist releases in response to 2-on-2 wrist grabs

   c. 13 out of 15 correctly executed wrist releases in response to 2-on-1 wrist grabs

   d. 12 out of 15 correctly executed wrist releases in response to 3 different grabs done in random order

Your Score =

   a. (#)_____ correctly executed 1-on-1 releases

   b. (#)_____ correctly executed 2-on-2 releases

   c. (#)_____ correctly executed 2-on-1 releases

   d. (#)_____ correctly executed releases to random grabs

2. Split-Focus Drill

In this drill you'll be splitting the attacker's focus with a strike just prior to your release attempt. These preliminary moves, sometimes called *distraction techniques*, are helpful in situations where you've already attempted a quick release and have been unsuccessful in breaking a powerful hold. Some defenders use this even before their first effort, having decided that a simple release probably won't be effective because of the strength of the attacker's grip.

Your choice of which distraction technique to use will depend on the availability of body weapons and the degree of force you feel is necessary to ensure your release. For instance, assume that an attacker has grabbed both your wrists using a 2-on-2 grip. In less threatening circumstances (when help is very close, or the assailant is skittish, nervous, ambivalent, etc.), a quick, sharp kick to the shins may be enough to cause the assailant to loosen his or her grip and enable you to break free.

In more threatening circumstances (when you're far from help, or the assailant is strong and sadistic), it's better to aim your kick at the knee where you're more likely to cause damage and incapacitation. If one hand is free (i.e., the attacker is using a 1-on-1 or 2-on-1 grip), you'll likely use it for a distraction technique, rather than risking a kick that may cause you to lose your balance.

The free hand is usually the furthest from the attacker, that is, your trailing hand. You'll recall that the trailing-hand strike is more powerful than a lead-hand strike because of the greater hip rotation. Using your trailing hand provides you with a powerful distraction technique and also puts you in a good position for the follow-up break.

Generally speaking, the degree of force you use and the target you select will depend on your assessment of what's necessary to ensure your escape. Depending on the particular wrist grab used, your options include using the available body weapons for throwing front-facing strikes.

In this drill, you'll practice a number of predetermined distraction techniques in response to all 3 grab variations. In each case, use the designated distraction technique (1 of the front-facing counterattacks), and then follow it with the appropriate release. You should develop a feel for the ease with which these front-facing counterattacks can be used in conjunction with wrist releases, when the situation warrants.

After practicing the designated responses, you'll have the opportunity to come up with a few of your own. As you create your own responses, remember that you want whatever distraction you use to flow easily into the appropriate break.

Success Goals =

a. 10 correctly executed front snap kicks to the shin followed by a quick wrist release in response to 2-on-2 grabs

b. 10 correctly executed front snap kicks to the knee followed by a quick wrist release in response to a 2-on-2 grab

c. 10 correctly executed palm-heel strikes with your free hand followed by a quick wrist release in response to either 1-on-1 or 2-on-1 grabs

d. 10 correctly executed web strikes with your free hand followed by a quick wrist release in response to either 1-on-1 or 2-on-1 grabs

e. 15 correctly executed distraction techniques of your choosing in response to any of the 3 grab variations

Your Score =

a. (#)_____ front snap kicks to the shin followed by wrist releases

b. (#)_____ front snap kicks to the knee followed by the wrist releases

c. (#)_____ palm-heel strikes to the nose followed by wrist releases

d. (#)_____ web strikes to the throat followed by wrist releases

e. (#)_____ distraction techniques of your choosing followed by wrist releases

3. Strike Follow-Up Drill

In some situations, you may be required to follow up a wrist release with a strike. The follow-up strike may be used to keep the attacker from resecuring his or her hold. Or, you may feel that a strike is necessary to discourage the assailant from pursuing you following a wrist release.

Throughout the following exercises, allow a margin of safety of 2 or 3 inches between your fully extended limb and your partner's body targets. In parts a, b, and c, you'll break the hold and follow instantly with designated follow-up strikes. These strikes include both front-facing and side-directed counterattacks, selected for the ease with which they can be used in conjunction with particular releases. Then, in part d, you'll have an opportunity to come up with follow-ups of your own choosing, after first gaining your release from any of the 3 wrist grabs.

The designated follow-ups are these:

a. A punch to the nose with your trailing hand following release of a 1-on-1 grab.

b. A hammerfist to the attacker's nose, temple, jaw, or neck following release of a 2-on-2 grab. This side-directed counterattack is possible because the powerful trunk rotation used to power your release leaves you with one side toward the attacker. That is, of course, the side from which the hammerfist is thrown.

  c. A side stomp kick to the knee following release of a 2-on-1 grab. Once again, a side-directed counterattack is made possible by virtue of the trunk rotation, used to add force to your break, carrying you into a side stance. The side stomp kick should be thrown toward the attacker's nearest knee.

  d. After effecting a release from any one of the 3 wrist grabs, select follow-up strikes of your choice.

Success Goals =

  a. 10 correctly executed punches to the attacker's nose following 1-on-1 releases

  b. 10 correctly executed hammerfists following 2-on-2 releases

  c. 10 correctly executed side stomp kicks following 2-on-1 releases

  d. 10 follow-up strikes of your choice following release from any grab variation

Your Score =

  a. (#)_____ follow-up punches

  b. (#)_____ follow-up hammerfists

  c. (#)_____ follow-up side stomp kicks

  d. (#)_____ techniques of your choice to follow wrist releases

4. Sandwich Drill

The purpose of this drill is to learn how to sandwich a wrist release between a preliminary move—such as a distraction technique—and a follow-up strike.

As in the previous drills, you'll be doing 3 designated distraction–release–follow-up combinations in response to each of the 3 wrist-grab variations. Then you'll once again have the opportunity to improvise and create your own ''sandwiches.''

The designated combinations are these:

  a. In response to 1-on-1 grab

> Distraction technique—lead-leg front kick to shin
> Release—1-on-1 release
> Follow-up—trailing-hand palm-heel strike

  b. In response to 2-on-2 grab

> Distraction technique—lead-leg front kick to shin
> Release—2-on-2 release
> Follow-up—Hammerfist

  c. In response to 2-on-1 grab

> Distraction technique—trailing-hand palm-heel strike
> Release—2-on-1 release
> Follow-up—side stomp kick to nearest knee

Success Goals =

a. 10 repetitions of designated response to 1-on-1 grab

b. 10 repetitions of designated response to 2-on-2 grab

c. 10 repetitions of designated response to 2-on-1 grab

d. 10 responses of your own choosing to random wrist grabs, incorporating both a distraction and follow-up technique

Your Score =

a. (#)_____ repetitions of response to 1-on-1 grab

b. (#)_____ repetitions of response to 2-on-2 grab

c. (#)_____ repetitions of response to 2-on-1 grab

d. (#)_____ responses of your choosing to random wrist grabs

Wrist Releases
Keys to Success Checklist

Have your teacher or practice partner critique your responses to the 3 different wrist grabs using the checklist items in Figure 13.1. In each case, be sure to maximize power against the weak link of the attacker's grip, the thumb. Ask the observer to pay particular attention to use of trunk rotation to power release, attack trajectories, and details of your grip. Finally, ask for feedback on the effectiveness and fluidity of movement in your use of both preliminary and follow-up moves.

Step 14 Recall Under Stress

Recall under stress refers to the critical ability to think clearly and strategically during a threatening or assaultive situation. While some people seem naturally to maintain presence of mind and good judgment under extreme pressure, this is also a skill that can be developed.

The drills in this step are designed to help you improve your capacity to stay focused on your defense, to make accurate observations regarding the nature of an attack, to adjust rapidly to changes in positioning and range, to select reasonable responses to different forms of attack, and, finally, to implement these responses in an effective, relatively calm, and disciplined manner.

WHY IS EFFECTIVE RECALL UNDER STRESS IMPORTANT?

Like many other emergencies, assaultive situations are frequently marked by confusion, panic, fear, and sometimes pain. In spite of this, you must maintain the necessary presence of mind to assess the situation, determine options and risks, and select and implement appropriate defenses.

HOW DO I IMPROVE RECALL UNDER STRESS?

Physical mastery of the techniques presented in Steps 4 though 14 is a good start. Once you're able to execute these skills powerfully and quickly in nonstressful practice situations, adding stressors can stretch your ability to remain focused and calm. The drills you've been practicing each step generally reflect a progression from least to most stressful and realistic. The drills in this step go even further in helping you train not only your body, but your mind and emotions as well.

Each of the first three drills in this step introduces increasing levels of spontaneity and unpredictability. Observational and judgment skills will be highlighted as you practice the self-defense techniques you've learned in previous steps in progressively more challenging contexts.

In "5-for-5," you'll be practicing your defense against predetermined, then random attacks from the same attacker, as you circle each other and maneuver for position. The precise moment of attack remains uncertain.

In "Challenge Line," you'll be defending against predetermined, then random attacks from a variety of attackers, adjusting to different body sizes, shapes, and limb lengths.

In the "Milling Drill," you'll be defending against an even greater variety of attackers coming at you with predetermined, then random attacks from various angles.

Work through these drills at a moderate pace, making sure your techniques are biomechanically correct and controlled. Work to remain calm, focused, and flexible as you adjust to a constantly changing scene.

The final drill, "Confronting Your Fear," calls for you to review the entire Continuum of Response in order to construct a hypothetical defense to use in those assault circumstances you personally find most disconcerting and frightening.

Recall Under Stress Drills

1. 5-for-5 Drill

This drill will help you develop greater skill in dealing with constantly changing angles of attack and with not knowing precisely when the attack is coming. Later in the drill, you'll practice responding appropriately to random (not predetermined) attacks.

Moving at slow speed, you and a partner maneuver around each other, taking care to remain approximately two arm's lengths apart. One of you, the designated attacker, attacks the other, the designated defender, with a prearranged attack (e.g., front choke attempt, wrist grab, punch, etc.). The same attack is repeated 5 times, with a few seconds of maneuvering and circling between each attack. You then switch roles and the new attacker attacks his or her partner using the same attack move 5 times. Continue trading 5 for 5 until both of you are consistently able to respond effectively, 5 out of 5 times, regardless of the changing angle of attack and the uncertainty of knowing precisely when the attack is coming.

In this manner, you and your partner work through 4 different predetermined attacks and defenses:

Attack	Defense
Lunging punch	Evasive sidestep
Attempted front choke hold	Flying wedge plus push-away
Secured front choke hold	Kick/flying wedge/palm-heel strike
Wrist grabs (any variation)	Quick wrist releases

Once you've practiced all 4 attacks and defenses using this format, repeat the drill with the attacker choosing his or her attacks at random. The defender must now quickly determine the nature of the attack (1 of the 4 already practiced) and respond appropriately. Continue trading 5-for-5 random attacks and gradually increase speed as the defender's skill in reading and responding appropriately to the incoming attack warrants. As you increase the speed of this drill, be especially careful to control your strikes, and do a restrained press in the flying wedge plus push-away. Continue until you're consistently able to defend effectively against all 5 random attacks.

Success Goals =

a. 5 successful responses to lunging punches

b. 5 successful responses to attempted front choke hold

c. 5 successful responses to secured front choke hold

d. 5 successful responses to wrist grabs

e. 5 successful responses to random attacks

Your Score =

a. (#)_____ successful evasive sidesteps

b. (#)_____ successful flying wedges/push-away

c. (#)_____ successful kick/wedge/palm-heel strike

d. (#)_____ successful quick wrist releases

e. (#)_____ successful responses to random attacks

2. Challenge Line

Caution: Keep a moderate pace in this drill.

You'll be defending against different attackers who will be using first predetermined attacks and then, later, random attacks.

The drill requires a team of about 5 people. One team member at a time stands approximately 15 feet out in front of his or her team members, who are lined up, one behind the other.

One at a time, each team member breaks from the line, moves quickly toward the person standing out in front, and launches a predetermined attack. Each successive attacker waits until the previous attack has been neutralized before initiating a new one. A safe practice is to wait until the defender makes eye contact before charging.

Remember that although the attacker changes, the attack remains the same until the defender has defended against each of the people in the line. Then she or he quickly goes to the back of the line. The person previously at the head of the line now becomes the defender and assumes the position out front.

Repeat this process until all team members have had a chance to stand at the front and defend against the same attack thrown by each of the others. When the original person is back out front, begin the process again with another predetermined attack. Repeat this process with each of the attacks listed:

Attack	Defense
Lunging punch	Evasive sidestep
Attempted front choke hold	Flying wedge/push-away
Wrist grabs (any variation)	Quick wrist releases

(Defender turns back to line for the next 2 attacks)

Mugger's hold	Release/elbow/kick
Rear bear hug	Kick/scrape/stomp/head butt

Finally, repeat the process with random attacks. Team members choose from among the attacks listed so that defender is not sure which he or she will have to defend against. To avoid confusion, attackers should select one of the three front-facing attacks, such as lunging punch, front choke attempt, or wrist-grab variation. Attackers should give obvious cues, so defender can easily read the attack. This can be accomplished if, before charging, the attacker

- indicates that a lunge punch is intended by placing a fisted hand in front of his or her shoulder;

- indicates that an attempted choke is intended by placing open hands in front of chest, in preparation for reaching; or
- indicates that a wrist grab is intended by keeping hands low and by his or her sides.

In this way, you, the defender, will become more skillful in reading cues suggesting the precise nature of the attack and in responding with the appropriate defense.

Success Goals =

a. 4 effective responses to lunging punch (assuming four attackers in each line)

b. 4 effective responses to attempted front choke hold

c. 4 effective responses to wrist-grab variations

d. 4 effective responses to mugger's hold

e. 4 effective responses to rear bear hug

f. 4 effective responses to random front-facing attacks (e.g., punch, attempted front choke, or wrist-grab variation)

Your Score =

a. (#)_____ effective responses to lunge punches

b. (#)_____ effective responses to attempted front choke hold

c. (#)_____ effective responses to wrist grabs

d. (#)_____ effective responses to mugger's hold

e. (#)_____ effective responses to rear bear hug

f. (#)_____ effective responses to random front-facing attacks

3. Milling Drill

You'll recall a much simpler version of this drill from "Step 4: Evasive Sidestep." In this exercise, all participants mill around randomly for 3 minutes and maintain a minimum distance of two arm's lengths from the others. During the 3 minutes, you'll defend against an increasing number of types of attacks from a variety of attackers.

Anyone can be an attacker or a defender. To attack, you point at another and shout, "You!" Both of you make eye contact and freeze. Then suddenly you rush forward with a shout and the defender takes appropriate defensive action. Both begin to mill again until one or the other is moved to attack or called to defend.

For the first 30 seconds, only 1 attack or defense is allowed. Then, every 30 seconds or so, another is added, until all of the attacks and defenses presented in the following list are incorporated. This way, defenders are required to deal with different attackers (1 at a time, however), and constantly shifting angles and types of attack. Begin moving at half speed and go from there, exercising good control throughout. Allow plenty of space for sudden changes of direction and increasingly rapid movement.

First 30 seconds: Lunging punch/evasive sidestep

Second 30-second period: Add front choke attempt/flying wedge-push-away chest press (*very* light) (Note: If attacker succeeds in securing hold, respond with a kick–flying wedge–palm-heel as practiced in Step 10).

Third 30-second period: Add mugger's hold (This is a surprise attack from behind. Don't bother shouting to get attention beforehand.)

Fourth 30-second period: Add wrist grabs/quick releases (all variations)

Fifth 30-second period: No new attacks, but front-facing counterattacks can be added to wrist releases

Sixth 30-second period: Slow down and improvise. Attackers can try different kinds of unarmed attacks not covered in this book. Defenders should draw on skills they've learned to figure out a tactical response.

Success Goal = Ability to select and implement effective defenses in response to approximately 90% of attacks during 3-minute milling period

Your Score = (est. %) _____ of attacks responded to effectively

4. Confronting Your Fear

You can practice this drill anytime and anywhere. It can be done alone or with a practice partner. One of the most effective moments to practice are those in which you're afraid, since doing this can be reassuring. It involves looking carefully at assault circumstances or situations that you find particularly disconcerting, and mentally rehearsing a detailed, complete, and successful defense.

You've probably noticed that often when you find yourself nervously looking over your shoulder as you make your way across a parking ramp (or down a city street, or through a deserted apartment lobby), you attempt to dismiss your fears or anxieties. You tell yourself that you're being silly or paranoid and try, usually without much success, to focus on something else. An empowering and useful alternative to denial or dismissal of these fears is to confront them—to examine them in greater detail with an eye toward how to most effectively defend against what you fear. This imaging exercise will nearly always leave you feeling confident about your ability to respond appropriately and effectively to an attack. This is a powerful and effective way to *rehearse for success*. This exercise, done periodically, can also serve as a reminder of all your options, as outlined in Figure 14.1, showing the abbreviated version of the Continuum of Response.

a. First, identify a specific assaultive situation (a particular route you have to walk on a regular basis, an acquaintance in whose company you're frequently uneasy, a set of circumstances such as dealing with an inebriated and coercive date) that is especially frightening to you. You might want to stick to unarmed assaults involving a single attacker, because situations involving multiple assailants and armed attacks haven't been covered in this book.

Secondly, recall what you've learned about the nature and common circumstances of various forms of aggression. Draw from your own experiences and readings as well as the information presented in "Step 1: Awareness." Think about what precautionary measures you might take to reduce your accessibility and vulnerability to this particular assault.

Now, imagine that despite your precautionary efforts, you find yourself in this particular threatening situation. Recall what's involved in evaluating any potentially assaultive situation (Step 2: Assessment). Quickly note pertinent details about the environment, the threatening individual, and yourself in your imaginary situation.

Now, determine the appropriate response (Step 3: Action). If this is a sexual assault situation, what stage has been reached? Is the potential attacker evaluating your victim potential? Is

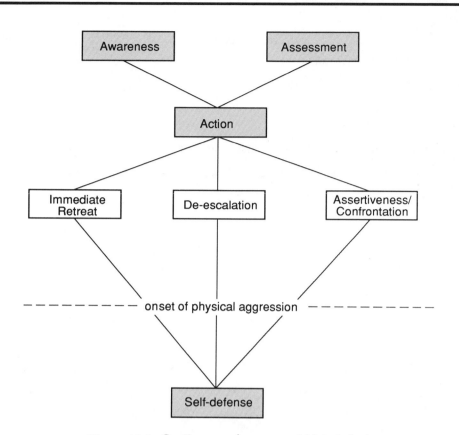

Figure 14.1 Continuum of response (abbreviation).

Assertiveness/Confrontation appropriate? Recall the verbal and nonverbal principles employed in this strategy and envision yourself implementing them effectively and confidently. Determine exactly what you would say and how you would say it. *"See" and "hear" yourself doing this* in your imagined scenario.

If this is not a sexual assault, but rather involves dealing with a highly agitated individual, will De-escalation tactics work? Recall the principles, verbal and nonverbal, and imagine yourself implementing these. Again, be specific and detailed in your imaginary situation.

See yourself decide that Immediate Retreat is called for, and note the circumstances and manner in which you could remove yourself from this threatening situation.

Finally, imagine that all your preventive efforts are unsuccessful and that the person in your imaginary scenario becomes physically aggressive. Again, be precise and detailed as you imagine this. Is the attacker punching? Where? Or grabbing? How? From what distance? How quickly?

See yourself in your mind's eye selecting an appropriate neutralizing technique, for example, evasion, block, or hold break. Determine whether a counterattack is necessary to get away, and then see yourself executing whichever strikes you determine are necessary.

Finally, see yourself retreating to safety, having effectively and successfully defended yourself in circumstances that hold a particular terror for you.

b. Having completed this mental rehearsal for successful defense, you might want to act it out with a partner. Give your partner the details of the attack and your response, then role-play the entire scene. This will further reinforce your grasp of options, help you recall the details of all 4 action strategies, and increase your confidence in your ability to keep yourself safe. It may also reduce, or even lay to rest, a longstanding fear.

Success Goals =

    a. Completion of imaging exercise

    b. Role-play the above with a partner

Your Score =

    a. _____ Completion of imaging exercise (yes? or no?)

    b. _____ Completion of role-play of above with a partner (yes? or no?)

Rating Your Total Progress

Throughout this book, you've been practicing a wide range of self-defense skills. Some of these have been more physical in nature, like, for instance, the foundational skills and their application in responding to particular kinds of attacks. At other times, you've worked on the mental, emotional, and verbal aspects of self-defense training. This has sharpened your observational, judgment, and communication skills in the practice of De-escalation and Assertiveness/Confrontation. Throughout this process, you've increased confidence, calm, and presence of mind in assessing danger, determining options, and implementing reasonable choices in dealing with the emergency of assault.

Each of the skills and capabilities presented in this book is listed in the inventory here. Read each item carefully, and then thoughtfully rate your progress.

PHYSICAL SKILLS

Developing a repertoire of basic techniques that can be applied to common attack situations is fundamental to learning self-defense. How do you rate yourself on the following skills and applications?

	Very good	Good	Fair	Poor
Foundational skills				
Evasive sidestep	——	——	——	——
Blocks	——	——	——	——
Front-facing counterattacks	——	——	——	——
Rear-directed counterattacks	——	——	——	——
Side-directed counterattacks	——	——	——	——
Applications				
Response to attempted front choke hold	——	——	——	——
Response to secured front choke hold	——	——	——	——
Response to mugger's hold	——	——	——	——
Response to rear bear hug	——	——	——	——
Response to wrist grabs	——	——	——	——

MENTAL, EMOTIONAL, AND COMMUNICATION SKILLS

These skills are most critical in assault prevention . . . enabling you to evaluate situations, anticipate danger, make appropriate judgments, and use your wits and words to push back that moment when a person you're dealing with becomes physically aggressive.

When preventive strategies fail and an individual becomes physically violent, these skills will enable you to remain focused and flexible. They increase the likelihood of your being able to make sound and instantaneous decisions in response to a constantly changing and often frightening scene. How do you rate yourself on the following mental skills?

	Very good	Good	Fair	Poor
Habits and routines reflect caution and concern with safety	___	___	___	___
Ability to project a vigilant and unvictimlike demeanor	___	___	___	___
Observant, quick to identify dangerous people and situations	___	___	___	___
Ability to assess situational factors and determine most appropriate preventive response	___	___	___	___
Ability to de-escalate a volatile situation	___	___	___	___
Ability to confront and be assertive with potential sexual assailant prior to physical aggression	___	___	___	___
Ability to think clearly and strategically during a physical attack	___	___	___	___
Ability to maintain calm and resist panic	___	___	___	___
Capacity for spirited and determined resistance, when appropriate	___	___	___	___
Self-belief and confidence in your ability to act effectively in your own defense	___	___	___	___

OVERALL SELF-DEFENSE PROGRESS

Given your answers to the previous questions, how would you rate your overall progress?

____ Very successful

____ Successful

____ Barely successful

____ Unsuccessful

Are you pleased with your progress?

____ Very pleased

____ Pleased

____ Not pleased

Name the three areas of greatest success for you in your self-defense training:

1. _____

2. _____

3. _____

Name the three areas in your self-defense training that pose the greatest ongoing challenge for you:

1. _____

2. _____

3. _____

Epilogue: The Next Step

WHERE DO YOU GO FROM HERE?

Now that you've acquired information and skills that will enable you to keep yourself safe in most threatening or assaultive situations, this Epilogue offers suggestions for keeping the self-defense skills you've acquired sharp through regular practice. For those of you who want more intensive and extensive training, the Epilogue presents information about the sometimes confusing array of martial disciplines available for study and offers ideas to those of you who want to join groups that work to reduce violence in this culture.

PRACTICING SKILLS PRESENTED IN SELF-DEFENSE: STEPS TO SUCCESS

If you're not likely to continue formal training in self-defense, consider setting aside a regular practice time to review the skills contained in this book. Practicing at least once a month will help you recall the techniques, if and when you need to apply them. More frequent exposure and practice will ensure that your techniques are fast, powerful, and effective.

From time to time, reread the first 3 steps, and note how well you've been able to integrate the precautions and preventive skills presented there into your daily habits and routines.

Another way to practice, of course, is to work through the ''Confronting Your Fear Drill'' (described in Step 14) on a regular basis. This mental rehearsal can be a powerful reminder of the range of options available to you in assaultive situations. It can also give you an opportunity to review the details of those options.

MARTIAL ARTS OPTIONS

Earlier in this book, I mentioned that self-defense is generally taught in schools and community centers, not as an *art*, but as a serious and practical skill. Self-defense training is usually eclectic in nature, drawing from such fields as criminal justice, conflict resolu-tion, crisis management, sociology, and psychology. The physical techniques that are taught, however, are almost always derived from one or more of the martial arts.

If you find yourself wanting to intensify and deepen your training in this area after completing this book, the next logical move is to find a good martial arts school. It has been said that short-term self-defense courses are to martial arts what first aid is to the field of medicine. You are now ready to go beyond the learning of a few practical skills and to invest in a serious and usually extended study of a martial discipline.

There are a number of different martial arts systems and styles. Plan on visiting a number of schools to observe a class or two and to talk with instructors about your particular goals before making a choice. You may find that you're drawn to a mat art, such as aikido or judo. Or the kicks and punches and blocks of karate may have a stronger appeal to you. You may find that you're not attracted to a particular art but are drawn to an instructor or the atmosphere of a particular school. Invest some time and thought in this decision in order to ensure that your experience is positive and productive.

To aid you in making this choice, here are brief descriptions of several different martial arts. Immediately following this section are some things to look for when evaluating a school and its instructor(s).

MARTIAL ARTS STYLES

Most martial arts originated in Asia, and their development has been heavily influenced by the Eastern thought and wisdom embodied in Confucianism, Buddhism, and Taoism. Various styles emphasize different qualities of movement and physical techniques but share a common goal of providing an arena for self-development and self-awareness. Common goals of martial training are to establish mind-body unity, self-confidence, discipline, self-control, fitness, longevity, and peace of mind.

Each art is, in and of itself, a complete system of self-defense.

Karate (kä RÄ tē)

Many different styles originating in Japan, Korea, and Okinawa emphasize a variety of hand strikes and kicks to vital points and a range of blocking techniques. Some schools are very traditional, teaching techniques and forms that remain relatively unchanged from the ones developed hundreds of years ago. Other schools and styles are more eclectic and committed to the ongoing development of a style. These people are generally more open to new training methods and techniques. And then, of course, many schools fall somewhere between highly traditional and eclectic.

Kung Fu (kŭng foo)

Originating in China, kung fu styles are much like karate in their emphasis on hand strikes, blocking maneuvers, and kicks, although the quality of the movement is more fluid and less linear. Some kung fu styles also emphasize pressure points, sweeps, and take-downs.

Jujitsu (joo JIT soo)

This is a very old and versatile Japanese art, emphasizing joint locks, pressure points, throwing, and falling.

Judo (JOO dō)

This is another Japanese mat art emphasizing throwing and falling, pins, locks, and other wrestling techniques. Judo is derived from Jujitsu and means 'the gentle way.'

Aikido (eye KI dō)

Meaning 'the way of harmony of the spirit,' this gentle art was developed by Ueshiba of Japan in the 1920s. This art aspires to the highest ethical standards, is entirely defensive, incorporating throws, pins, and joint-leverage techniques. It also emphasizes developing and controlling your own, or another's, *ch' i,* or 'life force.'

Tai Chi (tie CHEE)

The oldest of martial arts, tai chi originated in China thousands of years ago. A series of prearranged moves including deflections, strikes, kicks, parries, and balance techniques are usually done in a slow, meditative manner. Tai chi is considered an internal art and a form of meditation in motion. Although the movements and techniques are of a martial nature, today they're done more for exercise and fitness. However, the mental and physical skills you would learn in tai chi would certainly be useful in an assaultive situation.

Arnis/Kali (är NĬS/kä LĒ)

From the Philippines, these are stick-fighting arts involving the use of 30-inch rattan canes. Techniques learned with the cane can be adapted to empty-hand and sword techniques as well. These versatile and fluid arts also incorporates kicks, strikes, throws, and joint-leverage techniques.

Penca Silat (PĔN sä SĒ lät)

This art, which originated in Indonesia, incorporates movements and techniques similar to karate, as well as extensive groundfighting techniques, leg parries, and distinctive kicks.

Capolera (CĂ pō ER ă)

This Afro-Brazilian art was developed by African slaves and is usually done to music. The combination of martial movement with dance and acrobatic moves (cartwheels, handstands, etc.) was originally a means of disguising the art and preventing slaveholders from realizing that their slaves were practicing a martial art.

Ninjitsu (nĭn JĬT soo)

This art can be traced to feudal Japan and is sometimes referred to as 'the art of invisibility.' Early ninja were experts in most of the martial arts of the time (e.g., jujitsu and archery), as well as masters of disguise and illusion. This was fitting because they were also usually involved in spying and assassination. Authentic ninjitsu schools are hard to find in the United States, although many claim to practice this fascinating art.

SELECTING A SCHOOL

In addition to an affinity for the particular martial art being studied, there are other things you'll want to consider in selecting a school. For instance, what aspect of martial training does the school emphasize? Although most students learn martial arts for personal development, self-defense, and as a sport, different schools may place primary emphasis on a particular aspect.

For instance, some martial arts schools are oriented toward competition and participation in tournaments and contests. These schools often view their martial art primarily as a sport and focus less on other aspects.

Other schools will stress the practical application of skills to self-defense, while still others emphasize philosophy and spiritual growth and development. Knowing what you want out of your training will help you choose among schools with varying emphases.

The best way to get an idea of the orientation and emphasis of a school is to ask to visit a class. If visitors aren't allowed, check elsewhere. Most instructors will want you to know what you're getting into, and they'll encourage you to observe a class before enrolling.

When you visit the class, note the number and diversity of students. Is this a school that draws both men and women, kids and adults, athletes as well as people who are initially out of shape, people from a variety of backgrounds?

How long have instructors been training? Teaching? Are there female as well as male instructors? Does the instructor's attitude show respect, patience, and encouragement toward all students?

Does the school require you to sign a long-term contract? Are these financial terms you can live with?

Again, take your time in selecting a school and a style. Consider carefully what's important to you, then question instructors and students at the schools you visit to find out whether you're likely to achieve your personal goals there. This will be time well spent, and it will ensure that your experience in martial arts training is empowering, enjoyable, and useful.

OTHER OPTIONS

There are many ways to deal with the threat of victimization in our culture. You may seek an individual solution involving the study of self-defense or a martial art. That may be a wise and appropriate response, because it considerably reduces your own chances of being victimized. But it doesn't reduce the common threat of violence we all live with as a society.

If you're interested in working to reduce violent victimization on a larger scale, consider getting involved with community groups or projects addressing this issue. Most communities have at least some of the following groups:

- Rape Crisis Centers offer counseling and other services to victims of sexual assault. Generally, these groups provide educational programs as well to neighborhood, church, and school groups.
- Battered Women's Shelters provide shelter and all other necessities for battered women and their children.
- Child Abuse Prevention Services offer preventive and educational programs for kids, their parents, and teachers.
- Neighborhood-based groups address gang violence, theft, and other security issues.

If you're not a joiner—of either a martial arts school or a group working to reduce violence in our society—you can talk to friends and acquaintances about what you've learned. In particular, share information about the nature and circumstances of various forms of aggression. Help lay to rest the myriad misconceptions that surround crimes of violence and serve to increase vulnerability and risk.

Remember that self-defense is not simply a few tricks or techniques, but a lifestyle and general attitude of vigilance and preparedness. Knowledge of self-defense skills enables you to conduct the business of your life with peace of mind. So, take your Next Step, whichever you've chosen. Do it with the intention of living a full and a safe life.

Appendix

Individual Program

INDIVIDUAL COURSE IN _____ GRADE/COURSE SECTION _____

STUDENT'S NAME _____ STUDENT ID # _____

SKILLS/CONCEPTS	TECHNIQUE AND PERFORMANCE OBJECTIVES	WT* ×	POINT PROGRESS** =				FINAL SCORE***
		%	1	2	3	4	

Note. From "The Role of Expert Knowledge Structures in an Instructional Design Model for Physical Education" by J.N. Vickers, 1983, *Journal of Teaching in Physical Education, 2*(3), p. 17. Copyright 1983 by Joan N. Vickers. Adapted by permission.

*WT = Weighting of an objective's degree of difficulty.

**PROGRESS = Ongoing success, which may be expressed in terms of (a) accumulated points (1, 2, 3, 4); (b) grades (D, C, B, A); (c) symbols (merit, bronze, silver, gold); (d) unsatisfactory/satisfactory; and others as desired.

***FINAL SCORE equals WT times PROGRESS.

References

Amir, M. (1971). *Patterns in forcible rape.* Chicago: University of Chicago Press.

Blush, G. (1982). *Behavioral issues and strategies in dealing with disruptive and dangerous persons.* (Available from Gordon Blush, EDD, Target Productions, Rochester, MI 48063)

Borgida, E., & Brekke, N. (1985). Psychological research on rape trials. In A.W. Burgess (Ed.), *Rape and sexual assault: A research handbook* (p. 329). New York: Garland.

Burkhart, B., & Stanton, A. (1988). Sexual aggression in acquaintance relationships. In G. Russell (Ed.), *Violence in intimate relationships* (pp. 43-65). Great Neck, NY: PMA.

Finkelhor, O. (1979). *Sexually abused children.* New York: Free Press.

Graff, S. (Ed.) (1983). Self-defense teacher's guide. Proceedings of the National Self-Defense Teaching Practicum. Columbus, OH: Intrepid Clearinghouse.

Groth, N., & Birnbaum, J. (1979). *Men who rape: The psychology of the offender.* New York: Plenum Press.

Harlow, C.W. (1989, May). *Injuries from crime* (NCJRS Publication No. NCJ 116811, p. 6). Washington, DC: U.S. Department of Justice, Bureau of Justice Statistics.

Johnson, A.G. (1989). On the prevalence of rape in the United States. *Signs, 6,* 136-146.

Knight, R., Rosenberg, R., & Schneider, B. (1985). Classification of sex offenders: Perspectives, methods, and validation. In A.W. Burgess (Ed.), *Rape and sexual assault: A research handbook* (p. 222). New York: Garland.

Koppel, A. (1987). Lifetime likelihood of victimization (Bureau of Justice Statistics Technical Report No. NCJ 104274, p. 3). Washington, DC: U.S. Department of Justice, Bureau of Justice Statistics.

Koss, M. (1985, October). Ms. magazine campus project on sexual assault. [Funded by National Center for the Prevention and Control of Rape]. *Ms.,* p. 58.

Rodabaugh, B., & Austin, M. (1981). *Sexual assault: A guide for community action.* New York: Garland STPM Press.

Schuiteman, J. (1989). *Using confrontation to deter sexual assault.* East Lansing: Michigan State University.

Selkin, J. (1975, January). Rape. *Psychology Today,* pp. 71-75.

Spiro, J. (1988, July). *Self defense against weapons.* Seminar and notes presented at National Women's Martial Arts Federation Special Training, Geneva, NY.

Straus, M., Gelles, R., & Steinmetz, S. (1980). *Behind closed doors: Violence in the American family.* New York: Anchor Books.

Tavris, C. (1982). *Anger: The misunderstood emotion.* New York: Simon & Schuster.

United States Department of Justice, Bureau of Justice Statistics. (1988, March). *Report to the nation on crime and justice* (2nd ed.) (NCJRS Publication No. NCJ 105506). Washington, DC: Author.

United States Department of Justice, Law Enforcement Assistance Administration. (1976). *Queen's Bench Foundation's project rape response.* Washington, DC: Author.

Suggested Readings

On Self-Defense

Bart, P.B., & O'Brien, P.H. (1985). *Stopping rape: Successful survival strategies.* Elmsford, NY: Pergamon Press.

Bateman, P. (1978). *Fear into anger: A manual of self-defense for women.* Chicago: Nelson-Hall.

Caignon, D., & Groves, G. *Her wits about her: Self-defense success stories by women.* New York: Harper & Row.

Colao, F., & Hosansky, T. (1987). *Your children should know.* New York: Harper & Row.

Crum, T. (1987). *The magic of conflict.* New York: Simon & Schuster.

Elgin, S.H. (1983). *The gentle art of verbal self-defense.* Englewood Cliffs, NJ: Prentice Hall.

Funk, S. (1985). *Special fight: Common sense self-defense for the aged and disabled.* Dallas: Pacific Press.

Sanford, L.S., & Fetter, A. (1979). *In defense of our selves: A rape prevention handbook for women.* New York: Doubleday.

Tegner, B., & McGrath, A. (1976). *Self defense for your child: Practical defenses and assault prevention for elementary school age boys and girls.* Ventura, CA: Thor.

General Interest

Bass, E., and Davis, L. (1987). *The courage to heal: A guide for women survivors of child sexual abuse.* New York: Harper & Row.

Bolton, R. (1979). *People skills—How to assert yourself, listen to others and resolve conflict.* New York: Simon & Schuster.

Brownmiller, S. (1975). *Against our will: Men, women and rape.* New York: Simon & Schuster.

Haldane, S. (1988). *Emotional first aid: A crisis handbook.* Barrytown, NY: Station Hill Press.

Henley, N. (1977). *Body politics: Power, sex, and non-verbal communication.* Englewood Cliffs, NJ: Prentice Hall.

Pease, A. (1981). *Signals.* New York: Bantam Books.

Schechter, S. (1982). *Women and male violence: The visions and struggles of the battered women's movement.* Boston: South End Press.

About the Author

As an instructor of self-defense and a third degree black belt, Joan M. Nelson has over 20 years of active training in martial arts. She received her master's degree in health and physical education from Michigan State University and is the founder and owner of Movement Arts, Inc., a Lansing-based center offering programs and training in martial arts, personal safety skills, health education, and fitness.

Nelson has served as a consultant in personal safety skills training for a variety of public and private sector groups, including the Michigan Department of Corrections and western European self-defense instructors. She is a co-founder of the National Women's Martial Arts Federation and an active participant in anti-violence groups.